D0994115

The Dyslexia Handbook 2012

Edited by **Professor John Stein** and **Kate Saunders**
Managing Editors **Debbie Mitchell,**
Dominic Llewellyn-Jones and **Jane Flowers.**

Published by

The British Dyslexia Association
Unit 8, Bracknell Beeches, Old Bracknell Lane,
Bracknell, RG12 7BW

Helpline: 0845-251-9002
Administration: 0845-251-9003
Website: **www.bdadyslexia.org.uk**

Front Cover designer: Dianne Giblin

It seems the dyslexic ability to use 'visual language' is very much sought after nowadays and very possibly (along with our intuitive ability to cut straight through the 'maze' and find answers etc) make an important difference in the future for people.

I have 'survived' using 'the visual language' in many ways, all my life, also in drawing, painting, sewing etc. as an expression of who I really am. Although undiagnosed till I was 46, am now so busy 'creating' in one form or another, that I have far less times to think of the problems of being dyslexic (as I did growing up) I don't 'force' myself to do what I really can't any more, rather concentrate on being as good as I can where it's 'ok' for me.

ISBN 978-1-872653-54-9

9 781872 653549

£10.00 (inc P&P)

The British Dyslexia Association

The Dyslexia Handbook 2012

A compendium of articles and resources for dyslexic people, their families and the professionals who deal with them.

Edited by **Professor John Stein** and **Kate Saunders**
Managing Editors **Debbie Mitchell,**
Dominic Llewellyn-Jones and **Jane Flowers.**

British Dyslexia Association

Published by
The British Dyslexia Association

Editorial Note

British Dyslexia Association

The Dyslexia Handbook 2012

1. Great Britain. Education
2. John Stein
3. 978-1-872653-54-9.

Published in Great Britain 2012 Copyright © British Dyslexia Association 2012

Printed by Information Press, Eynsham, Oxford
www.informationpress.com

Advertising sales by Space Marketing
Tel: 01892-677740
Fax: 01892-677743
Email: **brians@spacemarketing.co.uk**

British Dyslexia Association
Unit 8, Bracknell Beeches, Old Bracknell Lane, Bracknell RG12 7BW
Helpline: 0845-251-9002
Administration: 0845-251-9003
Fax: 0845-251-9005

Website: **www.bdadyslexia.org.uk**

B.D.A. is a company limited by guarantee, registered in England No. 1830587
Registered Charity No. 289243

Contents

Introductions

Editors' Introduction

Professor John Stein

The B.D.A. handbook has been published every year since 1993. It has become an indispensible guide for dyslexic people, their parents and teachers. Most of what anyone needs to know in order to begin to help people with dyslexic problems in a truly practical way is contained in this one slim volume. I am particularly honoured to be helping to edit the 2012 edition because the contents show that we really are beginning to make headway with persuading the world at large that dyslexia is a real problem that is nevertheless remediable, not hopeless.

However these advances have unfortunately led to a kind of counter revolution. This has emerged for two reasons. First, despite dyslexia affecting all social classes equally, there is a widespread perception that middle class children gain an unfair share of resources because the middle classes can navigate the system better, armed with the B.D.A. handbook – in the words of the old adage: 'middle class children are dyslexic; working class children are thick'. In addition some dyslexia professionals have urged us to move away from definitions of dyslexia that emphasise the discrepancy between a child's reading and their oral and general intelligence towards a definition purely in terms of poor ability to translate letters into the sounds they stand for accurately and rapidly, ie lack of phonological skills. These two influences have unfortunately led some influential people to claim that dyslexia probably does not exist at all.

The argument runs as follows: all dyslexics lack phonological skills. Likewise all kinds of poor reader lack phonological skills. Therefore all kinds of poor reader may be said to be dyslexic, or none of them are. Furthermore since training in phonological skills helps both 'dyslexics' and other poor readers equally, there is no point in calling any of them dyslexic. Therefore, it is argued, dyslexia does not exist as a separate entity from other causes of poor reading. This is a flagrant example of what RH Thouless called the most common trick of dishonest argument, the 'undistributed middle'. Even if all poor readers do have phonological problems (which is highly debatable), only some dyslexics do so, and many have other features, such as visual problems, as well. These are what distinguish dyslexia from poor reading due to poor teaching, lack of opportunity, lack of family support etc. They include its genetic basis, which strongly indicates that dyslexia has a distinct neurobiological basis; this leads to the brain differences between dyslexics and good readers that have been repeatedly demonstrated. The most important distinction, practically speaking, is the great discrepancy between what you'd expect a dyslexic to achieve in reading on the basis of her oral skills and general intelligence compared with the very poor standard she actually does achieve in reading and spelling due to her dyslexia.

This is not just a boring academic argument; it threatens to impact seriously on diagnosis, teaching and the allocation of resources. Perhaps a quarter of adolescents in the USA and the UK leave school without being able to read properly. This is a potent cause of misery, loss of self confidence and, all too often, descent into criminality. A recent report from the KPMG Foundation suggests that the long term costs of illiteracy are c.£2500 per illiterate adult per year, ie perhaps £15 billion per annum in the UK (KPMG 2006), due to the unemployment, mistakes, extra education required and the criminal activity that it so often engenders. Many children can be helped to avoid illiteracy and cope with the modern world, if, with the help of this B.D.A. Handbook, their individual dyslexic problems are recognised early on and appropriately remediated. But many of them will be consigned to a life of unemployment and failure if the idea that dyslexia is a 'myth', and doesn't really exist, begins, against all the evidence, to become generally accepted.

What Is Dyslexia?

Dr Kate Saunders

Dyslexia is a Specific Learning Difficulty (SpLD) that affects around 10% of the population. In 2009 Sir Jim Rose's Report on 'Identifying and Teaching Children and Young People with Dyslexia and Literacy Difficulties'; gave the following definition of dyslexia. This was adopted by the B.D.A. Management Board, but with the addition of the further paragraph shown below, which should always appear with it:

The definition of dyslexia in the Rose report is as follows:

- 'Dyslexia is a learning difficulty that primarily affects the skills involved in accurate and fluent word reading and spelling.
- Characteristic features of dyslexia are difficulties in phonological awareness, verbal memory and verbal processing speed.
- Dyslexia occurs across the range of intellectual abilities.
- It is best thought of as a continuum, not a distinct category, and there are no clear cut-off points.
- Co-occurring difficulties may be seen in aspects of language, motor co-ordination, mental calculation, concentration and personal organisation, but these are not, by themselves, markers of dyslexia.
- A good indication of the severity and persistence of dyslexic difficulties can be gained by examining how the individual responds or has responded to well founded intervention.'

In addition to these characteristics, the B.D.A. acknowledges the visual processing difficulties that some individuals with dyslexia can experience, and points out that dyslexic readers can show a combination of abilities and difficulties that affect the learning process. Some also have strengths in other areas, such as design, problem solving, creative skills, interactive skills and oral skills.

Dyslexia is a one of a range of Specific Learning Difficulties (SpLDs). Also included in this umbrella term are:

- Attention Deficit Disorder (ADD)/ Attention Deficit Hyperactivity Disorder (ADHD)– this condition includes difficulty sustaining attention and ADD can exist with or without hyperactivity
- Dyscalculia – specific difficulty with aspects of mathematics
- Dyspraxia/Developmental Coordination Disorder – involving difficulty with motor coordination and organisation of some cognitive skills
- Dysgraphia– difficulty with fine motor skills, especially for handwriting
- Asperger's Syndrome – this includes difficulty with certain interpersonal skills and may be seen as the mild end of the autistic spectrum
- Specific Language Impairment

Some dyslexic individuals experience visual processing difficulties. These can include visual stress, visual tracking problems, binocular visual dysfunction and difficulty with visual-motor perceptual skills . They may mis-sequence and reverse letters or numbers, report that letters 'move', lose their reading across lines of print, be sensitive to the 'glare' from the white page/board/screen and find that their eyes tire easily when reading. These difficulties can also affect reading musical notation. Non-dyslexic individuals can also sometimes suffer visual stress symptoms.

Difficulty with phonological processing is a key issue for many dyslexics. Dyslexic individuals can have trouble hearing the difference between letter sounds (i.e. sound discrimination), linking letter shapes and sounds together, building strings of letter sounds up into words, breaking words down in to constituent sounds, understanding how word structure works, word retrieval and speed of processing.

Some dyslexic individuals also experience elements of another SpLD. These are referred to as 'co-morbid' or 'co-occurring' difficulties. In families where dyslexia is present, there can also tend to be a higher proportion of individuals with other Specific Learning Difficulties.

Early Identification is extremely helpful for dyslexic individuals, as it enables early intervention. The provision of well structured, multisensory teaching is generally recommended for dyslexic individuals. There is now a good level of knowledge about the types of teaching (both individual and class based), teaching resources and support methods/equipment that benefit dyslexic individuals (please see **www.bdadyslexia.org.uk**). Without these interventions, difficulties with the acquisition of written language skills can become exacerbated, giving rise to increasing frustration, for all concerned.

Dyslexia can be considered a disability, placing a duty on organisations to make reasonable adjustments and not to behave in a discriminating manner.

Throughout history, dyslexic individuals have been amongst those who have made enormously positive contributions to society (e.g. Albert Einstein, Leonardo Da Vinci).

Working together the B.D.A. and an increasing army of supporters are determined to bring about a dyslexia friendly world.

Contacts

For general help and enquiries about dyslexia go to the B.D.A.'s website **www.bdadyslexia.org.uk** for wealth of information about Dyslexia or call the National Helpline (10am to 4pm Monday to Friday, and from 5pm to 7pm on a Wednesday) from **0845-251-9002.**

References:

Rose Review (2009) 'Identifying and Teaching Children and Young People with Dyslexia and Learning Difficulties', DCFS Publications. Download from: **www.teachernet.gov.uk/ publications Ref: DCSF-00659-2009**

Saunders, K. & White, A. (2002) How dyslexics Learn: Grasping the Nettle.

PATOSS, Evesham.

The
MOATSCHOOL

An Aspirational Secondary Day-School
for Children with Specific Learning Difficulties

Founded in 1998 The Moat School is London's first co-educational secondary school for dyslexic children offering an intensive and structured learning programme teaching the national curriculum.

Children receive a totally inclusive education, they understand their difficulties, but thrive academically, emotionally and socially in spite of them. Pupils have individual timetables that address their needs, and creative talent is nurtured in small classes enabling success in public examinations. The Moat School is CReStED registered and has been described as the 'Gold Standard' in SpLD education.

The Good Schools Guide says: "Something special. Not for children wanting to be cosseted and comforted, but a hard-working haven for bright, determined dyslexics and dyspraxics who know what they want from life and will achieve when given a chance".

Come and see for yourself

Bishop's Avenue, Fulham, London SW6 6EG
T: 020 7610 9018   **F**: 020 7610 9098
office@moatschool.org.uk   **www.moatschool.org.uk**

Parents

Early Identification of Possible Dyslexia

Donna Grey

The early years of a child's life are recognised as a crucial stage. The Foundation Stage within our schools acknowledges the importance of this time and aims to maximise learning experiences, hopefully encouraging all children to reach their full developmental potential.

Despite recent cuts within our education system, the Government still recognises that a good Early Years education is critical to later achievement. As parents, we are informed of the skills and traits our children are expected to display at Nursery and Reception class level. Our pre-schoolers are expected to hit certain physical, intellectual, social and linguistic targets as they progress through their early years. Studies of the early years; defining what is 'normal development' and the promotion of strategies to encourage children to reach their development milestones, are many and varied.

All children are individuals and will develop at their own pace and there is therefore no clear dividing line between expected development and that which may be delayed. Within the early years, we are very conscious of labelling children before they have even had a chance to develop. Such labels can inhibit and create a 'self-fulfilling prophecy; the child begins to see herself as others see her ,rather than as an individual. In terms of dyslexia however, there is an increasing argument that we can, with sensitivity, identify some traits of dyslexia within the early years. The idea being that the earlier we identify these characteristics and take action, the better. Early years professionals know the physical, intellectual, social and linguistic skills expected of a child at each age and stage. We could therefore expect then, that certain traits that deviate from these expectations may suggest a problem.

Numerous academic studies advocate early identification and intervention. Miles and Miles stated: 'if dyslexic children are caught early, less time is needed for catching up, while in many cases they can be helped before frustration sets in'.

Jean Augur ('Early Help, Better Future') stated: 'It is now evident that there are many signs well before school age which may suggest such a profile and the consequent difficulties ahead. Parents and pre-school carers as well as educators in those early years are amongst those in the best position to recognise these signs, and to provide appropriate activities to help. Training in some of these activities will help to build firm foundations for later, more formal, training.'

The B.D.A. highlight the following characteristics within a pre-school child which may suggest dyslexia:

- Has persistent jumbled phrases, e.g. 'cobbler's club' for 'toddler's club'
- Use of substitute words e.g. 'lampshade' for 'lamppost'.
- Inability to remember the label for known objects, e.g. 'table, chair'.
- Difficulty learning nursery rhymes and rhyming words, e.g. 'cat, mat, sat'.
- Later than expected speech development.

Pre-school non-language indicators:

- May have walked early but did not crawl - was a 'bottom shuffler' or 'tummy wriggler'.
- Persistent difficulties in getting dressed efficiently and putting shoes on the correct feet.
- Enjoys being read to, but shows no interest in letters or words.
- Is often accused of not listening or paying attention.
- Excessive tripping, bumping into things and falling over.
- Difficulty with catching, kicking or throwing a ball; with hopping and/or skipping.

- Difficulty with clapping a simple rhythm.

A parent concerned that their child displays a number of the traits highlighted above should therefore discuss their concerns with their childcare professional. The B.D.A.'s Helpline can also be contacted if further support is needed.

The governments' recent proposed SEN and Disability Green Paper, also highlights the importance of early identification and intervention. The B.D.A., however, is concerned about Early Years professionals' knowledge of SEN: this needs to be enhanced through additional training. We support the commitment to utilise Surestart Children's Centres in early identification, however we are concerned that staff involved may not necessarily have sufficient knowledge of dyslexia. We therefore suggest that Surestart Centres become Dyslexia Friendly, through the B.D.A.'s Quality Mark scheme. This would ensure that all staff are appropriately trained and that practice is dyslexia friendly.

The paper also proposes replacing School Action and School Action Plus and their equivalents in the early years with a single category of SEN in early years' settings and schools. The B.D.A. is also concerned about this proposal. Since the introduction of Provision Mapping, the requirement to have IEPs for those Early Years children has been removed. It therefore becomes difficult to track a child's progress and to feed back to parents the child's attainments. SEN children may then 'disappear' from the school's list and this will have a negative impact on funding. Without School Action stage, children with dyslexia may have to fail profoundly in order for their need to be picked up at School. It may also make it more difficult to address their needs quickly. Early identification and intervention provides the best prognosis for dyslexic children (and is also the more cost effective policy – see Rose Review 2009).

The potential over-use of phonics to encourage emerging reading and writing skills is also controversial. Dame Clare Tickell's recent review of the Foundation Stage caused some debate about phonics. It was wrongly reported that her review contradicted the Government's current belief that phonics should still lie at the heart of early literacy learning and should be tested at 6 years. The Government plans to introduce a test of children's phonics skills in Year 1 as a stand-alone skill.

Dame Tickell stated:

'I have not recommended that phonics should be downgraded. Phonics is one of the most robust and recognised ways of helping children to learn to read and write. My report clearly highlights the importance of children starting school ready and able to learn, and I set out in the reading and writing goals the phonic development children should have reached by the age of five. The fact there is no longer a separate section labelled 'linking sounds and letters' does not mean I have deprioritised phonics'

Bernadette Duffy, head of Thomas Coram Early Childhood Centre and a member of the review panel, said phonics - the linking of sounds and letters - had been a successful strategy, but improvements in reading had lagged behind.

"If you look at the early-years foundation stage profile results, linking sounds to letters has gone up, but that has not necessarily been matched by a similar increase in children's reading," she said.

As experts discuss the Early Years and the expectations we place on our children, we must ensure we get the balance right. A child's emotional development is also key to fulfillment of potential. Dame Clare Tickell's review also identified playing and exploring, active learning and creating and thinking critically as the three characteristics of effective learning that are related to the key themes in early childhood development. As our knowledge of dyslexia develops and expands into the early years, we must ensure that all our children have access to these experiences.

Indicators of Dyslexia

Bernadette McLean

The shifting focus of definitions of dyslexia continues to alert us to the fact that we are dealing with more than a reading, writing and spelling problem. Recent definitions pinpoint difficulties with organisation, memory, word retrieval and speed of processing. Sir Jim Rose's definition stresses that the condition exists on a continuum ranging from mild to severe; thus we are unsurprised that not every dyslexic is identified in the early years. It is encouraging that most recent definitions emphasise the abilities and strengths of dyslexic profiles as well.

So, our picture of indicators of dyslexia may be different at different stages in the education of people with dyslexia. The lesson we learn from our increased understanding about timing and cerebellar difficulties in dyslexia is that we need to check out complications with timing, sequencing, naming speed and general levels of automaticity of skills over and above literacy difficulties. The environment will determine when and where these difficulties become apparent.

Moving from pre-primary to primary education, children may suffer information overload with too much listening and not enough doing. Listening and general receptive and expressive language skills need to be firmly in place before children are ready to learn literacy skills. Many children fail to learn phonics because the underpinning knowledge of phonological skills is not in place. During the primary years children are expected to make the transition from **learning to read** to **reading to learn.**

Other signs of possible dyslexia in the early years include;

- seemingly bright in many ways but slow to acquire spelling/reading/writing.
- late speech and language development
- pronunciation problems

- grammatical errors in speech

- word finding problems

- difficulty learning nursery rhymes and unable to give rhymes

- history of hearing problems e.g. earache and glue ear

- allergies e.g. hay fever, asthma

- confusing letters and numbers that are similar m/w, 6/9, etc

- difficulty learning tables and number bonds

- difficulty learning to tell the time and learning the language of time such as "ten past two"

- clumsiness in small actions such as handwriting or drawing, or in large actions such as learning to ride a bike or throwing and catching balls

- difficulties in learning letter formation and confusing upper and lowercase letters

- difficulties in learning spellings with omission of letters and syllables or using the correct letters but in the wrong order

- Poor attention or concentration for activities involving the reading, writing, listening

- problems remembering more than one instruction at a time

- difficulty learning the alphabet ,days of the week, months of the year

- difficulty learning the letter sound links

- difficulty detecting alliteration or giving words which start the same sound

- difficulties learning a sequence of activities such as tying shoelaces or doing up buttons

- yet often exceptional talents in creative areas such as drawing and playing with Lego

At secondary level, earlier difficulties may persist as well as new problems appearing, such as coping with the increased demands of the curriculum. They may show many of the following features:

Reading

- inaccuracies, for example when reading examination questions
- poor speed of reading
- poor skimming and scanning
- difficulty in getting the main idea
- difficulties coping with heavier reading demands
- reading silently may be easier for comprehension than reading aloud

Writing

- persistent spelling difficulties
- difficulties in copying from the board
- difficulty organising and structuring written work
- choosing simple vocabulary that is easier to spell
- difficulty in spotting errors and proofreading
- problems with legibility and speed of handwriting
- difficulty with punctuation

Listening

- problems with note-taking, unable to listen and write at the same time
- difficulty in following more than one instruction at a time

- difficulty with concentration and attention

Language

- verbally may be good, thus a discrepancy between oral and written skills
- word retrieval problems
- difficulty in acquiring topic words
- slow to answer questions
- unable to cope with fast verbal input, particularly if the sentence structure is complex
- more easily distracted by environmental noise

Organisation

- poor organisational skills, e.g. problems with remembering to bring the right equipment and materials, timekeeping and meeting deadlines
- problems coping with more homework and lengthier assignments; often unsure of the precise requirements of homework set
- difficulty in satisfying the demands of different teachers

General

- difficulties with short term memory
- more easily tired than peers because of failure to achieve automaticity with many everyday activities
- more prone to examination stress
- difficulty with studying languages, in particular, French
- often better at practical subjects where less reading and writing is involved
- low self-esteem, leading possibly to behaviour problems and truancy.

Warning

Parents may look at these indicators and be unduly concerned when they spot some of these features in their children. It is worth remembering the quotation below.

> "It is a most extraordinary thing, but I never read a patent medicine advertisement without being impelled to the conclusion that I am suffering from the particular disease therein dealt with in its most virulent form. The diagnosis seems in every case to correspond exactly with all the sensations that I have ever felt."
>
> Jerome K Jerome **Three Men in a Boat**

Tim Miles described dyslexia as a pattern of difficulties: observant parents might look out for the persistence of difficulties over a period of time but also consider other at risk factors such as a family history of similar difficulties as well as talents in mathematical, computer, design, musical, mechanical or creative fields.

It is also worth considering whether other barriers to learning may have caused or be causing difficulties, such as medical conditions, illness leading to absence from school, being young in the school year, lack of opportunities for developing literacy skills at home, such as being brought up in a bilingual family or having foreign carers. This is not an either/or situation, but these other factors should be taken into account.

Conclusion

Because dyslexia can exist on a continuum from mild to severe, difficulties may not be noticed in the early years, particularly with bright children who may be compensating for difficulties automatically. Sometimes these children may draw attention to themselves not through their difficulties, but through avoidance strategies such as a reluctance to attend school or unacceptable behaviour in the classroom. This is unsurprising as it is much easier to ascribe their failure to a lack of effort; children who are awarded A for effort and E for attainment will often consider themselves stupid. This can also happen through family dynamics where dyslexic children compare themselves with their younger siblings who seem to find achievement so much easier.

It is now generally recognised that people with dyslexia often have co-occurring difficulties such as dyspraxia and ADHD. Often the symptoms may look similar; for example the dyslexic pupil may look as if he has attention deficit when the explanation may well be that he is finding it difficult to attend because of the nature of the task he is dealing with.

There is still controversy over the visual processing problems that dyslexic pupils may have; in our experience, some dyslexics will manifest signs of difficulty which reduce their ability to deal with print easily. Probing visual processing is recommended in assessment; parents can easily experiment with blue or yellow or other coloured overlays or simply coloured plastic sheets available from stationers to explore whether this makes the reading process any easier for their children.

If you suspect your child may be having specific learning difficulties (SLD)

Anna Pitt

A child's parents are the most influential persons in her education. Often teachers have to cope with a class of up-to 40 at a time, so it is easy for the needs of an individual child to go unnoticed if she just 'gets by'.

As a parent, it is difficult to gauge whether your child is performing at her age level, and harder still to know if s/he is performing at the best of her potential; especially when she is your first child, or the youngest in the year group.

The way to detect Special Educational difficulties is by watching for discrepancies in your child's abilities. If she is skilled verbally, able to entertain with elaborate stories eloquently told, yet unable to construct coherent written sentences it might be worth investigating.

Teachers are your eyes and ears within the school. Too often the limited resources for children with SEN are 'blamed' on teachers who try their very best for the children they are teaching. Maintaining a good relationship with your child's teachers and school is therefore imperative to ensure that they receive the best support.

If you suspect your child has a specific learning difficulty:

- Your first port of call is the class teacher.
  - Ask their opinion
  - Ask them to monitor performance to check for progress
  - Ask what support your child is receiving in the school
- If your child is less than 7 years old:
  - Start collecting evidence of their progress
  - Possibly get eyes and hearing tested to ensure no physical barriers to learning

- ○ Additional phonics teaching may improve your child's acquisition of literacy
- Early Years / School Action
  - ○ Once it has been observed that your child is not progressing as expected s/he will be registered for school action.
  - ○ At this stage the child, her teacher and her parents will together develop an individual education plan (IEP) for the child
  - ○ The IEP will define specific goals and targets for your child to assist with their areas of difficulty.
  - ○ The IEP should be reviewed at least once a term to evaluate the targets met.
- Early Years Action Plus / School Action Plus
  - ○ Where school action has been tried and deemed insufficient to meet the needs of the child they can be elevated to the level of School Action Plus.
  - ○ Here the IEP is expanded to include support by internal and/or external specialists.
  - ○ At this stage the LEA evaluates whether a statutory assessment is required.
- Statutory Assessment
  - ○ This is performed by a specialist professional and includes recommendations to add to the child's IEP.
  - ○ Should the needs of the child be identified to be beyond the help of School Action Plus, the child may be recommended for Statementing.
  - ○ Despite having a Statutory Assessment not all children are necessarily appropriate for Statementing. Even if they are not, a full explanation must be provided and a description of how your child's needs will be met in school.
  - ○ The LEA should write to inform you if they are completing a Statement within 12 weeks of the beginning of the assessment.

- Statement of Special Educational Needs
  - ◦ The LEA must provide you with a list of state mainstream and special schools, in your area, that can meet the needs of your child.
- If you disagree
  - ◦ First discuss this with the school and the LEA
  - ◦ You then have a right to appeal to the Special Educational Needs Tribunal
  - ◦ Also talk to your local parent partnership service about these options.

Remember that the support that can be provided at each of the levels in a school is dependent upon the individual LEAs and their budgets.

As your child progresses through education don't forget that any required support should continue throughout their academic and occupational career. At University, students should be encouraged to contact their University Disability Office and seek DSA (Disabled Student Allowances) to maintain their performance at optimum levels. Once people have left education they are still entitled to support throughout their career. 'Access to Work' is a government grant scheme which provides finance to employers to continue support for employees with Specific Learning Difficulties.

Anna Pitt, *BSc, DPhil, CPsychol, SpLD APC*

Tips and Parent Advice

Lorraine Cole

Satellite Navigation – Destination …… 'Literacy'

Most of us have used Sat Navs. Given that many of us find reading maps a trial, I think they have done wonders for many a family holiday, and marriage, for that matter!

As a child dealing with dyslexia or as a parent trying to navigate a way through the complex and shifting landscape of dyslexia support and provision, the experience can be like trying to plan a journey when you can't read the map. The Sat Nav is there to help.

1   You need to have a plan: Where is your destination?

The first thing you need to key in is your destination. Children with dyslexia need to be clear about where they are going and to be satisfied that there is a point to getting there. As a parent, you need to help structure their journey. It's no use getting side-tracked by all the 'Points of Interest' along a route if you end up in a muddle and never arrive at your destination. Dyslexic children will do best if there is a clear structure to support their learning.

2   What multi-sensory functions help me?

You can decide on the input settings in your Sat Nav that work best for you. Do you want to hear the instructions at the same time as viewing the route in your journey? Or do you want to 'disable' the voice as you find it confusing, or maybe 'Jane's' voice is just getting on your nerves? Part of the success of the Sat Nav is the facility to personalise functions to suit individual preferences. Likewise, children with dyslexia learn most efficiently when able to experience new learning in a multi-sensory way. This includes visual, auditory, oral and manual (or kinaesthetic) channels of information or input. In general, we learn best by using a range of senses, from seeing, doing, hearing and speaking. Dyslexic children can use stronger sensory pathways to support less efficient channels. They definitely need all the Sat Nav functions on - to start with at least.

3   Am I making sense of the journey?

A Sat Nav is capable of both large map (2D) and bite-sized detailed (3D) views of a journey. The facility to zoom in or pan out is always available. Hesitant drivers will appreciate the simulated 'Route Demo' before they set off. They will also like the detailed 'Route Instructions', breaking down the journey street by street. Developing effective learning strategies for a dyslexic learner must accommodate their individual learning styles (whether it be 'big picture' or 'inchworm' step by step approach).

4   Repetition Helps: The more you travel a route, the more you are able to remember it

Children with dyslexia benefit from lots of 'overlearning'. That is, returning to an area already covered, to help reinforce and make the learning 'stick'. In the same way, using a Sat Nav when repeating a route should help you remember the roads you need to take in order to reach your destination. Quite simply, doing something again and again helps you to become secure and automatic in what you do.

5   Has the Sat Nav made you 'helpless'? - Have you become independent or just reliant?

You might have needed the auditory **and** visual input at the beginning. However, continually travelling along the same route will decrease the need for dependence on the Sat Nav's auditory and visual functions. You will have become more familiar with the route as your short term memory begins to transfer to your long term memory.

Soon, you no longer need the support of the Sat Nav and switch it off altogether. A word of warning though: drivers who stop paying attention to the route and let the Sat Nav take over completely will remain dependent on it.

Likewise supporting children in overcoming difficulties caused by their dyslexia should not be used to avoid independence in learning and thought. Dyslexic children need to be actively involved in 'thinking about their thinking' and to reflect on what strategies work best for them. In 'education-speak' this is commonly referred to as metacognition.

6   Keeping the Sat Nav Charged

Unless your Sat Nav is charged, it will be of no use to you. In the same way a child who is demotivated and fed up with negative feedback from his efforts in his/her schoolwork, or indeed from family members in the home, will also run flat and be incapable of 'performing'.

Planning for Learning

You may be familiar with a few of the recent catch phrases given to educational initiatives over the last few years such as –

"Every Child a Reader"

or

"Every Child a Talker"

But when it comes to supporting children in their own home setting, (and at the risk of sounding corny) the only thing that should be on our lips and in our hearts is –

"Every Child is a Child"

Whether children are dyslexic or not, they do not want to go home to parents who have mutated into teachers - (surely every child's worst nightmare!). Children want to come home to a place of security and love. A dyslexic child very often comes home exhausted with the effort of keeping up in the most basic of literacy activities. Facing an anxious parent, diving upon them to do 'sounds' and go over spelling lists the moment they come home is bound to be counter-productive.

Children invariably pick up on their parents' anxieties. The temptation to rush in and sort things out can be difficult to resist. This is especially true for a parent who despite all evidence to the contrary, is told by school that little Emily is doing "fine".

In setting out to support children with dyslexic difficulties in the home setting, as parents we need to understand that **all** children respond to play, novelty and a sense of achievement.

Understanding the Situation - A Dyslexic Profile Snapshot

A Typical Dyslexic - Is there such a thing? There are common characteristics which overlap but children with dyslexia do not come shrink-wrapped. They are unique individuals with their own set of strengths and weaknesses. Typical difficulties most easily recognised are with reading, spelling and writing. These are 'above the water line' and can be easily identified, whilst hiding below are the less obvious struggles with memory, processing speed and phonological awareness.

Big picture thinking, problem solving, good spoken language skills and natural creativity are just some of the strengths that a dyslexic child can show very early in their lives. The acknowledgement and celebration of a child's strengths is absolutely vital in building up self-esteem and motivation.

Overlapping Difficulties – Dyslexia is a specific learning difficulty (SpLD) which can co-occur with other difficulties. Parents should be aware of this as it will help to shed light on why their child struggles with areas of learning outwith recognisable dyslexia-type traits. In fact, SpLD is really an umbrella term under which the following associated learning difficulties can be included:-

- dyspraxia: motor difficulties
- dysgraphia: poor hand eye co-ordination and handwriting
- dyscalculia: difficulty with mathematical concepts and
- Attention deficit disorder or attention deficit hyperactive disorder (ADD or ADHD): poor concentration and/or impulsivity

Parents can often be presented with quite a confusing picture. However, the first step is to establish if their child has dyslexia, and then to see if there are any other areas which are acting as learning barriers. It's important to keep in mind that a dyslexic child will have many individual strengths and, if there are additional difficulties, they will not be insurmountable. All that is required is a bit of Route Planning and an understanding that there may be more Alternative Routes needed along the way.

Memory : Beyond Reading and Spelling

Parents will spend much time and effort supporting their child's reading and spelling. However, they may not realise that one of the reasons their child struggles so much is down to poor memory. Effective intervention and support in and out of school must address this fundamental area.

Tailoring support for a dyslexic child will depend on many factors such as :

- needs
- strengths
- interests
- age and stage of schooling

Working with the School

Parents have to learn the skill of being a good advocate for their child. They are in a better position than anyone to know if their child is avoiding homework because they want to watch a favourite TV programme, or whether their specific difficulties make it impossible for them to tackle it.

Unless your child is home-schooled, parents will need to work in as collaborative a relationship with the school as they can. Although there are exemplar dyslexia-friendly schools, there are others that have some way to go if they are to offer dyslexic children a positive educational experience. In such cases, parents can feel a sense of helplessness as to what to do to move things forward. Negotiating the shifting landscape of educational support and provision can be like having a Sat Nav with a very out of date map on it. One simple step forward, however, would be to share with the school a free download from the B.D.A.'s Dyslexia Friendly Schools Pack and ICT Supplement :

http://www.bdadyslexia.org.uk/quality-mark-and-accreditation/dyslexia-friendly-quality-mark.html

Happy Families - Keeping Motivation and Interest

Families who increase their awareness of dyslexia will be less judgemental and more understanding. Such families will have a better insight into why their child is unable to remember :

- more than two instructions at a time,
- how to spell 'your' one day but not the next,
- how to organise their school bag with the right kit, in spite of daily reminders

For a child with dyslexia, a happy and supportive family home life plays a significant part in ensuring that they stay expectant and positive in their ability to learn. They will need to have sufficient emotional resilience in order to overcome the learning obstacles faced and the will to seek out the strategies that work best for them.

Support and Structure – Just Part of Family Life

Whether learning is academic or life-skilled based, effective learning requires the ability to organise, prioritise and sequence tasks – all of which rely heavily on memory. Learning is not just about schoolwork. It starts from the cradle and continues throughout life. In time, a child is expected to pull their own weight in the day-to-day organisation of family business.

Quite naturally, parents will gradually introduce their children to a range of chores/tasks such as in :

- setting the table
- tidying the bedroom
- cleaning out the rabbit hutch

Parents will soon identify that their child (whether they know they are dyslexic or not) will struggle more with such everyday tasks than would normally be expected.

Routines and Scaffolds

Setting up routines and giving scaffolds to support memory and break down the tasks are very helpful to a dyslexic child. This support does not have to be very 'clever'; it really comes down to what a parent already knows and may, to a large extent, already practise. Some suggestions on how to help with schoolwork, organisation and daily routines are given below:-

TIPS FOR PARENTS

- Chunk new learning into bite-sized bits to aid memory
- Revisit new concepts/knowledge/skills
- See connections with what is already known
- Use interests to motivate
- Experiment with multisensory methods – what works best?
- Use Assistive Technology where possible
- Understand there will be good days and bad days
- Make learning concrete (number lines/'flexitables'/clapping syllables/identify sounds with counters)
- Little and often is best
- Visualise/verbalise ideas and or text
- Present in different formats – oral, pictures, text, models, bullet points, checklist, mind-map, powerpoint, recording, role-play.
- Encourage active learning – child to reflect on what works and what doesn't and why.

Organisation at Home – Help with Routines and Regular Activities

- Distraction-free space to help concentration
- Use recording device to support memory

- Visual timetable schedule (for home/school) ie tasks/chores/ homework
- Checklist for packing school bag/overnight bag
- Colour code paperwork/worksheets/folders
- Use In/Out trays

Homework / Classwork issues –

Minimise difficulties by ensuring homework is clearly recorded.

Liaise with school to find out support offered and offer suggestions such as :

- Class mate homework buddy – share phone numbers/email to check details
- Homework sent by email
- Homework checked by TA/Teacher
- Homework recorded into device
- Homework printed
- Homework completed using word processor
- Alternative formats accepted as evidence of learning

'Points of Interest' and Future Reference

Where to Start –

Organisations, Resources, Support

Users of the Sat Nav will be familiar with the 'Points of Interest' option. If a driver wants to know how to get to the nearest Car Park or Library, a quick touch of the screen and clear directions are given. For parents, there is little in the way of clear direction in terms of who to turn to for advice about assessment, what schools should be responsible for, resolving educational disagreements or specialist 1:1 teaching.

Parents must not despair though, as there is a plethora of support and information sources to look to. The tricky bit is in knowing where to start.

Local Dyslexia Associations

An excellent starting point would be to seek out the support of your Local Dyslexia Association (LDA).

As well as free support and advice, LDA's hold a list of specialist teachers working in the area. See -

http://www.bdadyslexia.org.uk/membership/directories/lda-directory.html

Parents' Frequently Asked Questions

The B.D.A. have a set of FAQ's with useful links which many parents find very helpful. Issues covered are wide and there are numerous useful links too. See:

http://www.bdadyslexia.org.uk/about-dyslexia/faqs.html

For a more comprehensive list of resources, organisations, and helpful information see First Step References for Parents*

'You have Reached Your Destination'

- Early Identification of needs
- Appropriate intervention

If these two areas are addressed, then parents should be optimistic about their children's future. Seeking advice from organisations such as the local Dyslexia Association and appropriately qualified specialists such as Educational Psychologists or Specialist Dyslexia Teachers will help parents to move things forward. Children do not need their parents to be experts in the field of dyslexia. What is important is that they increase their understanding of what dyslexia is and be sure to listen carefully to what their child is telling them.

Fastest Route

The Dyslexic Sat Nav has, unfortunately, no "fastest route" but it does reassure us that there is always a way round. It will be necessary to use the 'Alternative Route' option. The 'Roadblocks' to literacy are just that – barriers, commonly in the shape of poor working memory, phonological awareness and information processing.

Route Options

Thankfully, the 'Route Options'(bringing in the assistance of, for example, Specialist Teachers, Assistive Technology, multisensory learning and structured, phonic-based literacy programmes) are all highly effective in enabling a child with dyslexic difficulties achieve their goals.

The Dyslexic journey is longer and harder but often provides a deeper and broader learning experience that covers areas of the 'country' that would otherwise not be explored.

First step references for parents

Getting Help for your Child:

http://www.bdadyslexia.org.uk/about-dyslexia/parents/
getting-help-for-your-child.html

Organisations

British Dyslexia Association
http://www.bdadyslexia.org.uk

Dyslexia Action
http://www.dyslexiaaction.org.uk/

Helen Arkell Dyslexia Centre
http://www.arkellcentre.org.uk/

Helpful Books for Parents

*B.D.A.'s suggested Book list for Parents
http://www.bdadyslexia.org.uk/about-dyslexia/parents/
books-on-dyslxia.html

Dyslexia – A Complete Guide for Parents and Those Who Help them, by Gavin Reid, 2011
Publisher – John Wiley & Sons Ltd, ISBN 9780470973738

Understanding & Managing Dyslexia for Dummies by Tracey Wood and Katrina Cochrane, 2009
Publisher – John Wiley & Sons Ltd, ISBN 9780470741320

100 Ideas for Supporting Pupils with Dyslexia, by Gavin Reid, 2008
Publisher – Continuum International Publishing Group, ISBN 082649398

Dyslexia – A Parents' Survival Guide, by Christine Ostler, 1999

Publisher – Ammonite Books, ISBN 1869666134
www.dyslexi.html

The Dyslexic Child at School and Home by Wendy Goldup
and Christine Ostler, in Dyslexia in Practice, A Guide for
Teachers, 2000
Publisher – Kluwer Academic / Plenum Publishers, New York,
ISBN 0-306-46251-6

Study Skills and Homework

*Taking the Hell out of Homework – Tips and Techniques for
parents and home educators* by Neil Mackay, 2010
Publisher SEN Marketing, ISBN 9781903842096
www.senbooks.co.uk

*Help Students Improve their Study Skills – A Handbook for
Teaching Assistants in Secondary Schools* by Jane Dupree,
2005
Publisher David Fulton, ISBN 184312263-4
www.fultonpublishers.co.uk

Homework Tips

**http://www.bdadyslexia.org.uk/about:dyslexia/parents/
homework-tips.html**

Spelling

*Teaching and Learning Spellings - A guide to help anyone
learn spellings more easily,* The Helen Arkell Dyslexia Centre,
1999
Publisher The Helen Arkell Dyslexia Centre, 1999,
ISBN 0 948612 17 7

Reading

101 Ways to Help your Child Read, by Patience Thomson,
2009
Publisher Barrington Stoke, ISBN 9781842996713
www.quickreads.org.uk

Literacy Programmes

DIY Readers' Support Pack DVD For Parents- sound to letter links and early sound blending
http://store.dyslexiaaction.org.uk/p-166-diy-readers-support-pack-dvd-for-parents.aspx

Toe by Toe
http://www.toe-by-toe.co.uk/

Launch the Lifeboat to Read and Spell
http://www.robinswood.co.uk/back-catalogue/lifeboat-read-and-spell-scheme/

Alpha to Omega
http://www.pearsonschoolsandfecolleges.co.uk/Secondary/EnglishAndMedia/11-14/AlphaToOmega/AlphaToOmega.aspx

IT Based Programmes
Nessy Learning
http://www.nessy.com/

Wordshark
http://www.wordshark.co.uk/index.aspx

Touch-Typing
A multi-sensory computer based learning course

TTRS
http://www.ttrs.co.uk/

Games
Trugs- Teach Reading Using Games
http://www.readsuccessfully.com/

SWAP
http://www.gamzuk.com/products.htm

Stile Dyslexia
http://www.ldalearning.com/support-for-you/support-for-you/stile-dyslexia/

Technology

Explores hardware and software useful in assisting dyslexic people of all ages
www.bdatech.org.uk

ICT Suppliers

Software for use with children with dyslexia
http://www.r-em.co.uk

AssistiveTechnology

http://www.arkellcentre.org.uk/

Free Resource Website

http://www.woodlands-junior.kent.sch.uk/literacy/index.htm

http://www.dyslexia-parent.com/hints.html

SEN Resource Suppliers

Crossbow - Dyslexia teaching and learning aids, visual stress and phonics resources. http://www.crossboweducation.com/

Cambridgehouse

www.cambridgehouse-dyslexia.co.uk

Multi Sensory Learning

www.msl-online.net

B.D.A. Local Dyslexia Associations

Chris Hossack

With over 60 associations covering most of England and
Wales, help is at hand locally where you need it most.
Local Associations, each with their own charity status and
mostly run by volunteers, are able to offer help and support
to parents / carers and their children who have concerns
about dyslexia. Contact details are on the B.D.A. website -
www.bdadyslexia.org.uk

Many of our associations started life as Parent Support Groups
and have grown into full associations offering helplines,
assessment, training, support and meetings, as well as working
with local Children and Young People's Services to resolve
problems and improve the learning environment for the dyslexic
child.

Through helplines, many of the initial fears of what dyslexia is,
how it affects your child, what the school is going to do /doing
about it / or not as the case may be, and what some of the
terms mean, can be resolved. Local helpliners can often give
suggestions of schools which are more supportive of dyslexics,
knowing through experience, and calls from other parents, more
detail of the local scenario.

Many local associations have campaigned long and hard to
have dyslexia even recognised by education authorities in
the first place and, having achieved this first aim, now plan
to establish the ethos of Dyslexia Friendly Schools (DFS)
throughout the whole of the teaching community, giving not only
a better form of education for the dyslexic, but for all learners
throughout the school.

Many parents are just not aware of what the school is actually
doing for their child and it is only when formal meetings are set
up either with the form teacher or the Special Educational Needs
Co-ordinator (SENCo), that the full extent or not, in the way of

provision, is made clear. Often a member of a local association will be only too pleased to go with you to guide you in asking the right questions and understanding the answers. If help is not being provided, and there is a clear case of dyslexia, then trained befrienders can take things a stage further by taking the case up with the local authority to press for action.

Some associations offer assessment, or are able to recommend local practitioners who are able to provide a service in this way. In some areas the Special Needs Teaching Service will provide this service as part of their contract with the schools.

If your dyslexic child is not receiving adequate or differentiated help at school, the local association will often have names of tutors who they can recommend as being particularly helpful to dyslexics. Some associations provide after- school or Saturday workshops at which one -to -one tuition can really make a difference. The other great advantage of this is that learning with others who also find it difficult helps their self esteem, in understanding that they are not the only ones with a learning difference.

Many parents feel unqualified to help their child with their learning, but to reinforce suggestions made on the B.D.A. website, many associations run training days for parents to help them understand not only what dyslexia is, but how best to help. Others run drop-in sessions where specific questions can be addressed by other parents who have already been through the same sort of experience, as well as specialists to answer the tricky areas.

The use of specialist speakers at open meetings is often a way in which local associations can draw in not only parents who want to know more, but also teachers and other professionals who are not trained in dealing with dyslexia. Teacher Training courses have for far too long devoted minimal time to special needs, a situation which is being addressed at last. The topics covered may go much wider than just dyslexia, looking at dyspraxia, dyscalculia, and many other differences as well as other topics relevant to the world of dyslexia.

Recent road shows held in Wiltshire and Northampton have attracted large audiences of teachers, teaching assistants and parents, and were addressed by officers of the B.D.A. and TV personality Jonty Hearndon from Cash in the Attic, who has dyslexic children as well as being so himself. Other associations have organised one day conferences attracting key speakers from across the country and drawing an audience from right around the region, lifting the profile of both dyslexia and the association in the process.

Following recommendations from the Rose Report, many associations have been able to support teachers going on to do more specialised training partially funded by the government, by providing pupils to be tested and taught during their training.

With the increase in technology now available to help dyslexics, many associations will have a specialist on hand who can advise on what materials would be most appropriate for your child; many have copies of such programs as Word Shark and Number Shark on which they can practice before deciding to buy. Some associations organise technology fairs at which manufacturers will set up stands demonstrating their products, allowing further hands-on practice before making a purchase. With new products coming on the market all the time, help which seemed only a dream a few years ago is now a reality.

An association website is always a good place to start as this will provide further contact details, information about forthcoming events, and news of what is happening in the local area as well as, in some cases, activities to play on line which are helpful to young dyslexics (Details on the B.D.A. website).

Not all associations are able to cover all of the things which I have outlined above, some are very small, or more specialised in the sort of help they provide, however it is the local knowledge which is the valuable component which the national helpline (0845-251-9002) **helpline@bdadyslexia.org.uk** is less able to offer, but which is excellent on all general topics, as well as new legislation and other legal matters.

These associations are run mostly by volunteers, a majority of whom came in the first place to obtain help, and having received that help have stayed on to help others overcome some of the hurdles which they have encountered. So why not join your local association, not only to learn more but also to offer back some particular skill you possess? Average subscriptions are about £16.00, and you will receive Contact magazine published by the B.D.A. three times a year, which gives details of events around the regions, national events and campaigns, as well as updates on technology from the New Technology Committee (NTC). As a member of your local association you are automatically a member of the national body, B.D.A., giving you a vote at the AGM and a very warm invite to our annual Family Day at which there are lots of activities for the young, and talks and demonstrations for the adults; a real fun day out, recent locations having been York, Leicester and Oxford.

Why not join us and find out more!!

Inspirational Dyslexic Individuals

"HOW you learn is just as important as WHAT you learn!"

Henry Winkler

HENRY Winkler is a well known Hollywood actor, producer and director. He's most famous for a TV show called Happy Days, but now he is the author of the best-selling children's books, Hank Zipzer, the World's Greatest Underachiever. Hank, like Henry, is dyslexic and the books show how he uses his creativity and imagination to get round his learning challenges.

Henry and First News editor, Nicky Cox, will be doing their fourth tour of UK schools in October as part of their My Way! campaign, spreading the word that "HOW you learn is just as important as WHAT you learn."

FIRST NEWS has been running a campaign for a year called My Way! It's about getting people to understand that everybody learns in their own way. For some

people,school is easy, but for others it might be harder. The important thing we want everybody to understand is that the way you learn has nothing to do with how smart you are. Around six children in each class have learning challenges, but that doesn't mean that they won't be fantastically successful in whatever they choose to do. As My Way! champion, Hank Zipzer author Henry Winkler, says: "Every child has brilliance inside them. Their job is to dig it out and give it to the world."

FIRST NEWS is on the road again in October, with Henry Winkler as part of the My Way! campaign saying:

Why did you decide to write books for children?

When I was first asked to write books for children I said: "No, I can't, because I'm dyslexic." I have learning challenges. I was told I was stupid, lazy and not living up to my potential most of my life. And, when you're younger and you're told that, you believe it. It's part of your self-image. But I was introduced to Lin Oliver and, together, we hatched Hank Zipzer. "Hank" comes from my name, Henry, and "Zipzer" is a woman who lives on the fourth floor of the building that I grew up in. I thought it was zippy. I find it hard to write down the words so I walk round Lin's rug and talk while she sits at the typewriter. And that's how we write. If you find something hard, there is always someone who can help you out.

The books are funny. Where did you get your sense of humour?

I don't know. From God. Lin is also funny. And, my children have learning challenges because it's passed on, and Lin has a son who has a learning challenge. So we took the experience from everything that we knew. Hey, one out of five kids has some sort of learning challenge, right?

So this kid is funny and he's so smart and creative. In the first book he couldn't write an essay about his summer vacation to the Niagara Falls so he made a model of it instead. You see, there is always more than one way to do something!

Like Horrid Henry, we think Hank Zipzer would make a great movie.

Well, you know, that would be terrific. The books certainly make kids laugh in the UK and in America.

What was it like for you at school growing up with dyslexia?

I am in the bottom 3% in the country of America in academics. That's why the second book is called I got a D in Salami because I got a bad grade in everything but lunch. I was great at lunch! School was unbelievably hard for me. Teachers didn't know what dyslexia was at that time. So I was labelled a trouble maker. I was the class clown.

They didn't let me be in the school play because I had to have extra maths lessons. And I became an actor anyway! It's so important that kids are allowed to find out what they're good at and not treated all the same.

What would you say to children suffering with dyslexia or other learning difficulties at school nowadays?

All of you reading this have greatness inside you. And, it is your job to figure out what your particular gift is. Dig it out and give it to the world. Everybody has to understand that they DO have greatness in them. And the way that we learn – if we learn slowly, if it's difficult – has no relation to our intelligence. Just because we learn differently, that does not mean that we are not incredibly smart human beings. That's something I need every child to understand. Some people are academic, some are sporty, some are creative, some can act and some are good with their hands. All of these things should be celebrated equally.

As a young actor, was it difficult for you to read lines at auditions and learn lines?

Yes. It was not only difficult for me as a young actor, it's still difficult for me as an actor today. Reading is very hard. My eyes somehow don't track the page really well. Reading out loud, especially in auditions, was like climbing Mount Everest with no clothes on!

Can't you get those coloured sheets that go over the words to make it easier?

Do you know what? Those sheets didn't exist when I was at school – they're like different colours, right? There are so many things now that are helpful, but when I auditioned, I used to improvise. I would read it, instantly memorise it – or as much of it as I could – and I would make up the rest.

Are you looking forward to your next My Way! tour in October and where are you going?

I can't wait. We have the best time. This will be the fourth time I've visited schools across the UK. We've been to England, Wales, Scotland, Northern Ireland and Ireland. This time I think we're going south and west because we've not been down towards Devon and Cornwall yet. And, you know what; kids in Britain are the same as those in America. The only thing that is different is some of the words they use and their accent. But, from what I have seen from the children in the UK, every one of you is spectacular. Every one of you is different and, yet, we are all the same.

uDraw are the sponsors of your My Way! tour with First News. How did that come about?

uDraw is the perfect partner for us. Firstly, they're very lovely people. But, secondly, uDraw is exactly the sort of thing I'm talking about. It's a new way of discovering the creativity inside you. I have a great friend, Alfie, who is 11, who has dyslexia. Alfie has been very involved in the My Way! campaign in Britain. So he's got a uDraw and, although he finds it hard to write, you should see the creative stuff he's done with a uDraw in his hands. It works with a Nintendo Wii and I think there are new versions coming out for other consoles very soon. If you draw something you don't like, you can just click to undo your last stroke. And, when you're finished, you can watch your whole drawing being created from start to finish like a video. It's just great.

My Story

Alfie Smith

My name is Alfie and I'm 11 years old. I'm a regular kid who likes doing everything that kids my age do. There is only one thing that's different about me. I have a special way of thinking that affects my learning. It's called dyslexia.

I have always liked school, have tons of mates and I'm good at lots of things (Maths, Science etc) but then there is Literacy. I love reading books so the reading part isn't hard for me, but when it comes to handwriting and spelling I really struggle.

Before I knew about dyslexia I used to dread the times when my teachers said we had to do some writing. Everyone else would write sentences, paragraphs and as we got older, pages, but I couldn't do it. My mind had all the ideas of what to write but it seemed my brain couldn't tell my hand what to do. I could only write a little bit. Sometimes teachers would tell me off for not trying hard enough and I would have to stay in at playtimes to do more. I can remember one of my friends seeing my writing one day. They told me it wasn't very good and that I should practise more. I was really sad inside because I felt that even if I practised it wouldn't get any better.

Homework was never much fun if it was spellings or writing. Mum and Dad always tried to help me too, but we often ended up having arguments. Sometimes Mum and I would argue until we both cried. She thought I was being lazy, but I was trying my hardest. I just didn't know how to make her understand.

When I started year 4 at school (about age 9) Mum and Dad say that I turned into a monster child! I was sad, angry and mad a lot of the time at home. It was because school work was getting harder and I felt rubbish at it. I just couldn't do it. My teacher at the time, though, realised that I was struggling and started to work out what might be happening. She guessed that I might be dyslexic.

I know that the school spoke to Mum and one day we sat down to talk about it. I kind of understood that it might be a good thing knowing that I have dyslexia, but I was scared. I didn't know about dyslexia and didn't know what it would mean;what treatment I would get; would I miss loads of lessons at school? Would I be away from my friends a lot? I was scared in some ways, but at the same time it made me feel really happy and relieved because I wouldn't get told off as much and would be getting more help in a separate lesson.

When I found out about being dyslexic, I started to find out about other people who are (or were) dyslexic too. I learned that lots of very famous and successful people are dyslexic just like me – Einstein and Winston Churchill are my historical favourites. I had heard about them and how great they were even before I knew they were dyslexic. Knowing that such important people in history were dyslexic gave me confidence in the early days of finding out that I'm dyslexic too. Surely if they could achieve great things, so can I. I sometimes dream that I could be as successful as modern day dyslexic business men like Richard Branson and Lord Sugar!

I think it's really important to have role models in life. To me a role model is someone who inspires me, motivates me and someone I can look up to. Just knowing that there are people that have learned to understand and work with their dyslexia (or mine) means that I know that I am not alone. Some of my role models are dyslexic and some are not.

I have been lucky enough to meet and get to know Henry Winkler OBE. He is dyslexic and didn't find out until he had already become famous as The Fonz. How he learned his lines and created such a great character is amazing. Henry is also a film director and now even writes books about a dyslexic boy, based on some of the things that happened to Henry as he was growing up himself. Pretty astounding for someone who went to school and thought they were only good at eating their lunch!

Henry always says that there is someone great inside even you and it's exciting to see who or what that's going to be. Someone

I know is dyslexic and he is a great plumber – he won lots of awards as an apprentice and now is very successful within a large national company at quite a young age. He didn't even find out he was dyslexic when he was at school. For me, he is a first class example of Henry's message.

Mr O was a Teaching Assistant who worked with me when I first found out about my dyslexia. He is my twin (our birthdays are on the same day) and he really, really understood what it was, and still is, like for me. He taught me spelling in "my way" of learning and we practised handwriting in a way that made sense to me. Mr O gave me so much time and understanding that I would not have achieved so much at school without him. I simply don't know if he is dyslexic or not but to me it doesn't matter. He is so great that he is a first class role model to me.

With the support that my role models gave me (even the ones that I have never met) I was able to start to work with my dyslexia and I now think of it as a "friend". We don't always get on, my mate dyslexia and me, sometimes it pushes me and challenges me in ways that I can't yet understand or work around, but life is certainly not as bad as I thought it was going to be 2 years ago. Those literacy lessons aren't as terrifying as they once were (it's still not my favourite subject and may never be, but I can get through the lesson now and understand what's going on). I did really well in my SATS at the end of year 6 at school and although I worked hard, I'm sure that each of my role models played a part too.

I wouldn't go so far as to say I'm an angel – I'm a boy after all! – but at least Mum and Dad understand too and home is a great place to be again.

When I leave school I'm not sure yet what I want to be. Maybe a cop, maybe an archaeologist (I've studied Egyptology since I was five), perhaps a marine biologist, maybe an actor (I'm really good at drama and expressing things). One thing for sure is that I want to be a dyslexic spokesman. I want to speak out and let people know being dyslexic is nothing to be worried about – it just means you have a different way of thinking, learning and doing things. If you start to understand your dyslexia, you can find ways of working things out, often better than other people around you. Perhaps if my message helps just one person or family maybe, just maybe, I could become a role model to other dyslexic kids myself.

Dyslexia my friend and foe

Jonty Hearnden

At school, and for the past 30 years of my working life, I have tried my best to hide what I considered to be an embarrassing and debilitating affliction. It was only after a chance meeting with Sir Jackie Stewart at one of my children's schools that I realised it was time to confront my own skeleton in my closet.

I have spent as long as I can remember concealing the fact that I have reading difficulties and writing issues. For more years than I care to remember I've tried to write as little as possible and certainly never to write if being observed or watched. When I do put pen to paper, I become panicked, angry and frustrated as I know what I write will become muddled and riddled with spelling mistakes. My paranoia and disability has stopped me from writing books, articles and even postcards - it even manages to prevent me from enjoying a good book on holiday as my reading speed is so slow – I cannot remember when I last truly completed a novel.

I am the one in ten of the population who has the hidden disability of dyslexia. Although diagnosed at around the age of 10, little was known of the condition and, although I was supported by some sympathetic teachers, I left with few O-levels and A-levels - insufficient to take me on to further education. Like many dyslexics, I left the sanctuary of school with little self-confidence in my ability to achieve anything academically and, as such, dreaded the thought of finding employment - filling in forms, writing introductory letters and a CV. However, I was fortunate at nineteen to get a job at Bonham's, the auctioneers in London.

Since this first introduction to the world of Art and Antiques, I have remained loyal to the industry that gave me my first job. However, it has not been plain sailing - I have spent most of my working life trying my best to hide my disability. Wherever possible, I sought the protection of sympathetic secretaries or if not, would take work home to be helped by family and select friends. I'm sure, like so many with dyslexia, I tried and succeeded in the most part to disguise the fact that writing a letter or reading a document was, and still is, an excruciatingly difficult task; however, as my career progressed, I found more and more ways of concealing it.

About twelve years ago, I was asked to join the panel of experts on the BBC flagship show "Antiques Roadshow", followed by many other antique related shows including "Cash in the Attic" and more recently "Put Your Money Where Your Mouth Is", where it is my knowledge of antiques and ability to work in front of a camera, not my writing expertise that is required. TV is an area I have thoroughly enjoyed, as what matters is my natural enthusiasm for the subject and not my ability to read, especially as I am never required to read a script or autocue and for that I'm eternally grateful.

Dyslexia is often hereditary and as such it appeared from an early age that my twin boys, who are now twelve, suffer from it. One twin in particular suffered so badly that the decision was made to send him to a special school to help with his learning disability. As a well-known dyslexic, Sir Jackie Stewart was asked to open a new building there and I remember clearly being moved to tears by what he had to say. He spoke eloquently of his own experiences, his difficulties with reading and writing, but what struck me most was his positive message about dyslexia. He talked about the way dyslexics often think - that dyslexics think "out of the box" and see things differently to many people and how they can be gifted with either creative talents or show prowess as sportsmen and sportswomen. He concluded by saying how these gifts could, and should, be used to the dyslexic's advantage.

For the first time I could see that being a dyslexic could be of benefit and that it was not necessarily a burden or embarrassment, but a gift. I left feeling emotionally drained, but elated - I had spent so long trying to deal with the frustration and loneliness that it was now time to share my experiences and to help others with the same condition. Still too many children with dyslexia are left languishing and disenfranchised at the bottom of classrooms. Teachers, parents and children themselves need to understand the positive side of dyslexia and the gifts children with the condition can offer the world. Too many dyslexic children and adults are left with low self-esteem and regarded as not intellectually equal to those who have no trouble with the written word - this should not, and does not, have to be the case.

A couple of years ago I was persuaded by a friend to go back to college, to a business school in fact, and to train as an Executive Coach. Initially terrifying, I found the journey incredibly stimulating and extremely rewarding - helping people develop and move forward, or help them facilitate personal changes in their lives, has been enlightening. The course lasted a year and at the end I was required to submit a five thousand word dissertation discussing my journey as a coach. Not surprisingly, this awful challenge was for me, at times, a good enough reason to quit the course and not bother to complete, as I just could not see how I was to achieve the final hurdle. However, during the time on my course I was fortunate to be introduced to the lovely people at the British Dyslexia Association and, whilst at a drinks party at the House of Lords hosted by Lord Addington (a keen supporter of the Association), I was introduced to Nasser Siabi. Nasser runs, and is a founder member of, a successful software company called Microlink PC, specialising in assistive technology for people with disability.

After several months had gone by still pondering my dilemma, I finally rang him and told him of my predicament. He immediately invited me to his offices near Southampton and suggested I try dictating my words rather than typing them into my laptop. He also suggested I try a mind mapping software called Inspiration, as well as another useful piece of kit called Read and Write. He also reassured me that instead of me having to pay for this amazing life changing equipment and software,the government had funds to assist Companies with this kind of software and training.

I immediately applied and within a short space of time found myself with headphones on and talking to my computer! Whilst it was a little tricky to begin with and reminded me of the feeling I had being in a radio studio for the first time, it was not long before I started to see the words flow onto the page and soon any anxieties turned into private elation.

On reflection, I have no idea how I could have ever written my dissertation without the assistance of this software. I now use Dragon Speak whenever I can - I find it most productive when writing e-mails and letters and have since equipped my two sons with this supportive software. I have also enthused to friends who I know suffer from dyslexia about my new found freedom and sometimes wonder how many people out there who suffer from this debilitating condition are unaware of the technologies available to help. I also wonder how many businesses are unaware that they employ people with a hidden 'skeleton'; if only they had access to this technology how much more productive would that business and those people be.

Good companies invest in and nurture what is most precious to them, the people that work there.

Jonty Hearnden has recently finished series 18 of Cash in the Attic and series 4 of Put Your Money Where Your Mouth Is. He can be contacted through his website, Jonty Hearnden and associates **www.dorchesterantiques.com**

Co-occuring Difficulties

Teaching Children with ADHD

Fintan O'Regan

Students with ADHD often challenge teachers in 3 main areas:

1. Activity level
2. Attention span
3. Impulsivity

Dealing with the activity level

Whether it is controlling their body or their minds some children appear to leap about all the time; unlike other children, it seems they are unable to control their motion on and off.

How to teach them to control themselves can be a difficult process but strategies do exist and they can be fun as well.

One technique for younger children to help them sit still is called "playing statues" (O'Regan, 2008). The child is asked to sit like a statue for a certain time which can be increased gradually, and shown on a bar chart or rewarded by stickers etc. In essence it is about helping the child to focus their attention and to control their bodies. Using a stopwatch to time them they will gradually learn to reduce their activity level. Being self taught this technique will often provide a long term solution.

Variations on this game are "Catch me if you Can" (O'Regan, 2008) and playing "Beat the Clock". These can be used to limit extraneous movement and focus tasks against a set of expectations for working in the classroom or during a time limited activity.

With older students much longer periods of sustained controlled activity can be achieved. We call this 'endurance training' and it involves lengthening the time and improving skills in sitting still in a variety of settings.

As a result the child will often need to have the session broken down for them. For example in a 40-minute lesson:

Part 1 - would consist of the teacher giving 10 mins introduction to the lesson about sitting still. After 10 mins she would indicate part 1 is over; part 2 begins

Part 2 - to focus on a task until the group discussion. Teacher then indicates this is over; move on to part 3.

Part 3 - to keep still during the group discussion. Teacher then says move on to part 4.

Part 4 - to keep it together during the clear up time. Teacher indicates the lesson is nearly over

All of these games or techniques to harness activity level will need to be practiced. Feedback of success or failure on the initial trials will be crucial to improve long-term outcomes.

Improving attention span

Although being hyperactive and impulsive is not helpful, without doubt the most important issue is poor attention span; this is the most damaging problem for the children. Lengthening this will be crucial for improving long term educational success (O'Regan, 2002). The first step is to acknowledge that we cannot assume that a child understands what paying attention really is; some children simply do not know what this is.

As a result a series of role-play activities between you and the child may need to take place. For example, during a taped story you, the supervisor, would show a series of examples in which you failed to attend and therefore didn't hear or understand what the story had been about. The child would then be asked why you didn't hear the story and to rate your listening skills. In addition you need to show how day dreaming interferes with understanding by reading something else while the taped story is on. Get the child once again to rate your performance in a detective type way.

Once you feel the child understands what we mean by paying attention, then we can start to teach attention span by timing his performance on a chart or similar visual tool. If the child is younger then you will often have to do the timing for them, but if they are older then they should be able to do it themselves.

Attention cards can be put on the child's desk or even computerized checks made. You want to hook the child into the learning situation by giving him or her the means to monitor their own performance on a regular basis during each learning activity. In many ways you are distracting the child in a proactive way.

Impulse Control

For some children impulsivity is the greatest problem and may lead to significant and often negative impacts. Once again the first stage in management is to explain the concept of impulsivity to a child who acts instinctively in many situations. Though he appears to be a risk taker, in his own eyes he was not taking a risk but driven by a reflex over which he had little or no control.

Explaining impulsive behavior may be easier with some children than others. The best place to start is to consider recent examples of impulsive incidents and explore with the child how these incidents might have been handled differently.

Getting the child to consider a number of separate situations and listing impulsive acts compared with thought out ones is an important exercise.

For example;

Impulsive Act	Thought out act
Running into street	Pausing at curb, checking for traffic
Interrupting conversations	Saying excuse me and waiting your turn

In essence to overcome impulsivity we need to consider teaching the child a hesitation response, in order to provide time for thinking before acting.

Again the way of doing this with younger and older kids will be different but essentially we have to sell to them the idea that they can control their own impulses.

In terms of day-to-day management of students who have these traits in the classroom, tried and trusted strategies are listed below. In some cases this will simply confirm good practice; but, as always, the key is to keep consistent with an overall plan to help them control their impulsive behaviour, yet to remain flexible as regards the minor distractions and incidents that will inevitably occur (*O'Regan 2005*).

- Seat the child near teacher but include him as part of the regular class
- Place him at the front with his back to the rest of the class to keep other students out of view.
- Surround him with good role models, preferably those seen as "Significant others". Encourage peer tutoring and co-operative learning.
- Avoid distracting stimuli. Try not to place the child near heaters, doors or windows, high traffic areas, the noisy air conditioner.
- Some children do not handle change well so avoid transitions, changes in schedule, physical relocation, disruptions. (Monitor closely on field trips)
- Be creative! Produce a "stimuli reduced area" for all children.
- Maintain eye contact during verbal instruction.
- Make directions clear and concise. Be consistent with daily instructions.
- Simplify complex directions. Avoid multiple commands.
- Make sure the child has fully understood before beginning a task.
- Repeat in a calm, positive manner, if needed.
- Help the child to feel comfortable with seeking assistance (most children won't ask)

- These children need more help for a longer period of time than the average child. Gradually reduce assistance.
- Require a daily assignment notebook. Make sure child writes down the assignment and both parents/teachers sign daily for homework tasks
- Give one task at a time but monitor frequently.
- Modify assignments as necessary. Develop an individualised programme,

The key elements in teaching rule governed behaviour management is to limit the rules to key areas of basic health and safety issues and basic black/white instructions, in terms of safety, physical/verbal behaviour, uniform and timekeeping.

Other tips are: be as specific as possible and use multiple prompts to get rule training operating; once again when possible provide immediate feedback on the outcome. Also ensure rules are over learnt and reinforced with consistent use of positive and (negative) consequences

Some children are not really rule breakers; they just cannot filter out the demands of environmental stimuli, all of which become priorities for their attention. Unlike traditional learners who, if the teacher is talking to them, can and do ignore a chair being scraped behind them, these children are too easily distracted by it.

As a result in the mind of an easily distracted child everything in their environment is equally important to attend to. Hence the first principle to overcome this is to train them to prioritise where to focus their attention in different circumstances. We have to help them to beat the distractions that take their attention away from the rules of engagement.

Teaching the child to overcome distractions is not an impossible task but it is going to take time. This is due to the fact that before the child can ignore them he or she needs to identify key elements before blocking them out and provide alternative filtering strategies so that distractions lose their attraction.

One way of starting this process is for the child to make a list in each class of which distractions cause his task completion or behaviour to be affected. With younger children this may entail help from an adult; but once this has been done there may be distractions that can be removed or at least adapted to some extent. It may also be useful to identify if visual or auditory distractions are the most intrusive. Next it is often useful to record the strength of the distractions and the time they take away from the main objective (*O'Regan, 2008*).

One method of beating distractions is the 'distraction zapper', which is a method of turning unwanted distractions into a game of recording successful attempts to ignore them and concentrate on their priority tasks. The zapper could be constructed as an imaginary laser gun for younger children or suitable age appropriate device for older children …to blow the distractions away and record how many hits you get, as in a laser quest game.

Teaching this by role-play with supervisor and child can yield excellent results; but, as always, learn by trial and error what works best for each individual child. Don't expect perfection; it will never happen!

Fin O'Regan

References

O'Regan F (2008) The Small Change 2 BIG DIFFERENCE series Hyperactive, Inattentive and Disorganised, Special Direct

O'Regan F (2002) How to teach and manage children with ADHD: LDA a division of McGraw-Hill

O'Regan F (2005) ADHD : Continuum International

The 'whole child' with developmental disorders Co-occurring disorders

Professor Amanda Kirby

Introduction

There is extensive evidence that developmental disorders such as Attention Deficit Hyperactivity Disorder (ADHD), Developmental Co-ordination Disorder (DCD - also known as Dyspraxia), Dyslexia, Specific Language Impairments (SLI), and Autism Spectrum Disorder (ASD), rather than being categorically separate diagnoses are in fact on a continuum and commonly overlap greatly with one another. Despite this knowledge there remain difficulties delivering UK-wide, consistent, interdisciplinary approaches for children with these diagnoses. A poignant review of integrated and inter-professional working from Galvani and Forrestor (2010) warns that 'users' "cannot be treated as bundles of complex problems each of which needs separate specialist input, but need a holistic service able to deal with such complex issues" (p3).

Terminology

Nearly twenty years ago, Caron and Rutter (1991) highlighted that a failure to attend to co-morbid patterns may lead to misleading conclusions by researchers, and negative intervention results from practitioners. This remains as true today as then. If children and their families remain in separate diagnostic 'boxes', moving from service to service to be assessed, this is not only an injustice to them, but also it has potential cost and time implications for effective delivery.

The oft-used term 'comorbidity' is confusing. One definition of this is: "The presence of co-existing or additional diseases with reference to an initial diagnosis or with reference to the index condition that is the subject of study. This is two or more 'diseases' with separate and different aetiologies which can present simultaneously or sequentially" (Perrin & Last, 1995).

However, as this term implies a separate aetiological basis for each of these disorders it may not be the appropriate term to use, as increasing evidence has shown that in some disorders there may be a shared genetic basis. An example is the shared genetic basis for some forms of specific language impairment and dyslexia which has been reported (Bishop & Snowling, 2004).

Other terms used include: 'co-occurrence' i.e. an accompaniment: an event or situation that happens at the same time as or in connection with another. This can imply causal relationships; 'co-existing' i.e. existing at the same time; and 'overlap' i.e. coinciding partially or wholly. It may be the latter term is a better one to be used when referring to these associations.

Evidence of overlap

With any developmental disorder, overlap is the rule rather than the exception, and several authors have highlighted this (eg Kaplan *et al*, 1998). The authors demonstrated that in a population of children with DCD, ADHD, and dyslexia overlap occurred frequently, with nearly 25% of those with one developmental disorder found to have all three, 10% both ADHD and DCD, and 22% both dyslexia and DCD.

A few of the many other examples of overlap include:

- DCD and ASD (Green et al, 2002; Dewey et al, 2007)
- DCD and ADHD (Rasmussen & Gillberg, 2000)
- ADHD and ASD (Sinzig et al, 2009)
- ADHD and reading difficulties (August & Garfinkel,1990; Kadejso & Gillberg, 2001)
- ADHD, dyslexia and mathematical difficulties (Mayes & Calhoun, 2006)
- Language disorders and behaviour(Ripley & Yuill, 2005)
- Language disorders and dyslexia (Snowling et al, 2000)
- Language disorders and DCD (Hill et al, 1998)

- Tourette's and ADHD (Shady, Rulton & Champion, 1988)
- Emotional and behavioural difficulties and dyslexia, ADHD (Place et al, 2000)

Explaining the reasons for overlap

Most developmental disorders are behaviorally defined and the aetiology is complex. They are caused by the interaction of multiple genetic and environmental risk factors. Some of these disorders are also co-heritable. A number of researchers have developed models to explain this complex and interacting mesh of influences, including Sargeant's 'Cognitive-energetic model' (2000) and Morton's 'Causal Modelling' (2004), describing different levels of interaction at biological, cognitive and symptomatic levels.

Implications for health and education provision

In order to support a complex group with a 'continuum of risks' Harley et al (2003) describe needing a 'continuum of service options' organised around individual interventions. This should reduce obstacles and go beyond the jurisdiction of each agency. Despite the knowledge of overlap, health and education services deliver widely variable models of practice across the UK and are often putting together local solutions and restrictive 'rules' for entry and exit. For example in some areas child and adolescent mental health services (CAMHS) lead ADHD and ASD services, and in the same area a paediatrician cares for children with DCD and other disorders, but not ADHD. Pathways into services from education can vary extensively and may include self-referral, defined pathways or an informal process via the GP or educational psychologist. Some limit provision by age despite extensive evidence that developmental disorders are life-long conditions.

Moving forward: Developing a developmental pathway

A potential approach to the management of developmental disorders is to provide common clinical and educational pathways. The need for inter-disciplinary, inter-agency, input

The Dyslexia Handbook 2012   75

into their diagnosis and management is in line with current emphasis on the importance of partnership working. The Special Educational Needs (SEN) Code of Practice (Department for Education and Skills, 2001), for example, highlights the importance of agencies working in partnership with each other. It suggests that partnership working should be based on a number of principles including:

- early identification
- continual engagement with the child and parent(s)/guardian(s)
- focused intervention
- dissemination of effective approaches and techniques
- integrated high quality, holistic support focused on the needs of the child
- a flexible, child-centred approach to service delivery

The need for effective information sharing and communication between agencies both at management but also at practitioner level is also emphasized.

Pathways for delivery

One example of pathways for children with ADHD, ASD and DCD has been developed in Swansea by Salmon et al (2006). They describe filtering processes acting as a funnel towards appropriate support (Sloan et al, 1999) and likened this to the SEN graduated response. Their three pathways are described separately but have some common themes. First, both health and education jointly developed the services. The process begins with the school identifying and providing an initial level of support and seeing whether this is adequate. The school also has a clear role in information gathering before health services are engaged. The health professionals, as well as providing clinical support, provide training in schools and for parents.

Other examples of developmental pathways include the 'Mid Cheshire ADHD pathway' (Burgess, 2002) which is similar to the Swansea ADHD model with a filtering process where referrals pass to the community paediatrician and a school nurse, based in a local clinic for a baseline examination.

What do the pathways have in common?

a) A shared ethos of responsibility.

b) Listening to concerns from parents or teachers.

c) Inclusive practice within the school setting.

d) Clarity of the pathway starting in education e.g. working with Special Educational Needs Coordinators (SENCOs).

e) Local solutions, from an evidence base for specific areas of difficulty e.g. reading, writing.

f) Referral to a local clinician(s) for first stage assessment only after information has been gathered from home and school and school based intervention has been tried and evidenced.

g) A two way system of information, advice and feedback.

h) Ongoing training.

i) Shared notes between services with some cases of parent held records.

Intervention

Providing a range and mix of service delivery options is essential. Direct intervention is not likely to be the only way to support children with developmental disorders, as realistically there are insufficient numbers of professionals to provide this. Indirect work can take a variety of forms. Specialist interventions need not always be direct, and direct interventions do not always mean that the child needs to be present. Several studies have also demonstrated the value of school/home based interventions.

Parents as partners and experts on their own children

Parents have a right to be key partners at all stages of the pathway and are not only essential for delivering successful outcomes but provide a cost effective approach, as they are usually motivated to try to make a difference to their children and also they have expert knowledge of their own children.

Conclusions

The wealth of evidence supporting the common ground between developmental disorders has implications for identification through to intervention and support. A move is indicated away from a targeted approach to an individual difficulty, towards a more holistic and integrated one. In the first instance this move can best be facilitated by adopting a common terminology.

Research has also shown that developmental disorders represent a complex continuum caused by a range of environmental and genetic factors requiring an interdisciplinary, inter-agency, approach to diagnosis and management. Indeed the call for separate agencies to work in partnership with each other to provide a service centred around the needs of the individual child has been highlighted as a priority in a number of government documents from both health and education (Department for Education and Skills, 2004; (Department of Health, Department for Education and Skills, 2004).

Parental involvement is essential in this process and can give great insight into the child's difficulties providing much more detailed information than a snap-shot assessment in one place and time. The partnership between professional and parent, coupled with the engagement of the child in the identification and intervention process, should not be an 'add on' but regarded as both an essential and cost effective approach to service delivery, especially given that developmental disorders are far more than 'just' of paediatric concern but are acknowledged as having a life-long impact.

References

August G & Garfinkel B (1990). Comorbidity of ADHD and reading disability among clinic-referred children. *Journal of Abnormal Child Psychology*, **18**(1): 29-45.

Bishop DVM & Snowling MJ (2004). Developmental dyslexia and Specific Language Impairment: Same or different? *Psychological Bulletin*,**130**: 858–886.

Burgess I (2002). Service Innovations: attention deficit hyperactivity disorder- development of a multi-professional integrated care pathway. *Psychiatric Bulletin*, **26**: 148-151.

Caron C & Rutter M (1991). Comorbidity in child psychopathology: Concepts, issues and research strategies. *Jour of Child Psych and Psych,* **32**: 1063-1080.

Dewey D, Cantell M & Crawford S (2007). Motor and gestural performance in children with autism spectrum disorders, developmental coordination disorder, and/or attention deficit hyperactivity disorder. *Journal of the International Neuropsychological Society*, **13**: 246-256.

DfES (Department for Education and Skills) (2001). *Special Educational Needs Code of Practice*. Nottingham: DfES Publications.

DfES (Department for Education and Skills) (2004). *Removing Barriers to Achievement: The Government's Strategy for SEN*. Nottingham: DfES Publications.

DoH/DfES (Department of Health, Department for Education and Skills) (2004). *National Service Framework for Children, Young People and Maternity Services, Executive Summary.* London: DH Publications.

Galvani S & Forrester D (2010). Integrated and inter-professional working: A review of the evidence. University of Bedfordshire.

Green D, Baird G, Barnett A, Henderson L, Huber J & Henderson S (2002). The severity and nature of motor impairment in Asperger's syndrome: a comparison with Specific Developmental Disorder of Motor Function. *Journal of Child Psychology and Psychiatry,* **43**(5): 655–668.

Harley D, Donnell C & Rainey J (2003). Interagency collaboration: reinforcing professional bridges to serve aging populations with multiple service needs. *Journal of Rehabilitation,* **69**(2): 32-37.

Hill E, Bishop D & Nimmo-Smith I (1998). Representational gestures in developmental coordination disorder and specific language impairment: Error types and the reliability of ratings. *Human Movement Science,* **17**: 655-678.

Kadejso B & Gillberg C (2001). The comorbidity of ADHD in the general population of Swedish school-age children. *Journal of Child Psychology and Psychiatry,* **42**(4): 487-492.

Kaplan B, Wilson B, Dewey D & Crawford S (1998). DCD may not be a discrete disorder. *Human Movement Science,* **17**: 471-490.

Mayes SD & Calhoun SL (2006). Frequency of reading, math and writing disabilities in children with clinical disorders. *Learning and Individual Differences,* **16**: 145-157.

Morton J (2004). Understanding developmental disorders: a causal modelling approach. Blackwell Publishing, London.

Perrin S & Last C (1995). Dealing with comorbidity. In: Eisen A, Kearney C Schaefer C (Eds.), Clinical handbook of anxiety disorders in children and adolescents, New York: Jacob Aronson Press.

Place M, Wilson J, Martin E & Hulsmeier J (2000). The Frequency of Emotional and Behavioural Disturbance in an EBD School. *Child Psychology and Psychiatry Review,* **5**: 76-80.

Rasmussen P & Gillberg C (2000). Natural outcome of ADHD with developmental coordination disorder at age 22 years: a controlled, longitudinal, community-based study. *Journal of the American Academy of Child and Adolescent Psychiatry*, **39**: 1424-1431.

Ripley K & Yuill N (2005). Patterns of language impairment and behaviour in boys excluded from school. *British Journal of Educational Psychology*, **75**: 37–50.

Salmon G, Cleave H & Samuel C (2006). Development of multi-agency referral pathways for attention-deficit hyperactivity disorder, developmental coordination disorder and autistic spectrum disorders: reflections on the process and suggestions for new ways of working. *Clinical Child Psychology and Psychiatry,* **11**(1): 63-68.

Sargeant J (2000). The cognitive-energetic model: an empirical approach to attention-deficit hyperactivity disorder. *Neuroscience and Biobehavioural Reveiws*, **24**(1):7-12.

Shady G, Fulton W & Champion L (1988). Tourette Syndrome and educational problems in Canada. Neuroscience and Biobehavioural reviews, **12**(3-4): 263

Sinzig J, Walter D & Doepfner, M (2009). Attention deficit/ hyperactivity disorder in children and adolescents with autism spectrum disorder: symptom or syndrome? *Journal of Attention Disorder,* **13**(2): 117-26.

Sloan M, Jensen P & Kettle L (1999). 'Assessing the services for children with ADHD: Gaps and opportunities'. *Journal of Attention Disorders,* **3**: 13-29.

Snowling M, Bishop D & Stothard S (2000). Is Preschool Language Impairment a Risk Factor for Dyslexia in Adolescence? Journal of Child Psychology and Psychiatry, **41**(5): 587–600.

What is dyscalculia?

Dr Steve Chinn

When I started to teach dyslexic students in 1981, I had no idea that many of my students would have difficulties with maths as well as language. I started investigating this problem thirty years ago and am still working away at it. Since then the word 'dyscalculia' has slipped into the vocabulary of education, with far less controversy, so far, than happened for dyslexia. Maybe that is in part down to how illiteracy has a much worse image than innumeracy. If you confess to not being good at maths you tend to find you are in quite a large club.

After years of being almost neglected, dyscalculia is beginning to attract more research. A definition is now in existence, though I am sure it will evolve just as the definition of dyslexia has evolved.

Dyscalculia is a condition that affects the ability to acquire mathematical skills. Dyscalculic learners may have a difficulty understanding simple number concepts, lack an intuitive grasp of numbers, and have problems learning number facts and procedures. Even if they produce a correct answer or use a correct method, they may do so mechanically and without confidence. (Department for Education and Skills, 2004)

You will notice that the definition focuses on numbers, on early arithmetic and not on higher levels of mathematics such as algebra. This makes sense as we are looking for problems that occur very early in the development of maths topics, rather than a sudden difficulty with, say, calculus. But, we have to remember that the early work sets the foundations for future developments, for example, addition develops from counting on in ones, multiplication develops from the repeated addition of numbers.

If learners do not understand numbers in those early stages then they are not likely to learn number facts. A combination of poor retrieval of facts and poor number sense has a hugely negative influence on learning mathematics. Children begin to fail and failure depresses motivation.

What might cause concern.

Can they recognise numbers and know what they represent?

There is a problem with an almost over-familiarity with the symbols we use for numbers. Children may be doing the number equivalent of 'barking at print'. Young children learn to count and learn that there is a set sequence for the numbers verbally and symbolically, but they may not connect or relate the words and the symbols to the quantities they represent. So, for example, given a choice of patterns:

Can they point to 'four' when they hear it, '4' when they see it? Can they recognise seven? Can they see that it is five and two more, five add two? Can they see '5'? Can they see that five is four plus one more? Can they see that 4 is five with one taken away? Can they see that ten is two lots of five? That ten is two 'times' five? That five is half of ten?

The games we play can teach much about early maths ideas, about number sense, rather than just about recognising number symbols. These questions are also about the operations (add, subtract, multiply and divide), about inter-relating numbers, about what is 'bigger' and what is 'smaller'.

For these games all you need are objects, say bottle tops, preferably bright coloured ones. The questions must be handled in a low stress, even a no stress way. The 'bigger or smaller' comparison is less judgmental (and also introduces the idea of estimation).

All this is about supporting memories, that are often less effective, by building understanding.

Are they confused by the vocabulary for the first examples of two digit numbers?

People, whether children or adults find security when things are consistent. Also we try to see patterns to help us remember and understand information. The bottle top or coin patterns for numbers 10 to 30 are consistent. You can show the pattern. Unfortunately the vocabulary does not support the pattern. In fact it confuses it. In English, 12 is said as 'twelve' which tells you nothing about the number. In Cantonese (translated) it is said 'one ten and two' which does tell you about the number. In English we say 'thirteen' and later 'twenty three'. In Cantonese the pattern continues, 'one ten and three' and 'two tens and three'.

And we use 'thirteen' and 'thirty', sixteen' and 'sixty' which sound very much alike to a new learner.

Confusion, and we have to understand how it may arise, can sow the seeds of doubt in a child's mind. My informal, but extensive survey of teachers across the UK reveals that too many children are giving up on maths as early as 7 years old. They need less failure and more success to be motivated.

So what do we do?

There is more than enough research to convince us that the curriculum needs adjusting so that it works for the children in the bottom 20% of achievement in maths. At least it should convince us. Children will only learn if we teach them in ways that lead to success, that is, ways that work for them. Sounds familiar? I did say that dyscalculia is a little behind dyslexia in being understood.

Materials and manipulatives will only work in the hands of teachers who know how to use them appropriately. I belong to the 'more the merrier' school of material users. What that means is that I like a whole range of 'stuff' so that I can pick what works for children and for the maths. We need to use the right visual support, the right language and vocabulary, the right amount of information so that short term and working memories are not overloaded, and we need empathy and a clear understanding of what it is we are teaching.

There is much good practice around, but .... as Prof Tim Miles said, (well, paraphrased a little), whilst most children survive and even learn whatever we throw at them, bad practice is disastrous for dyslexic (and dyscalculic) learners.

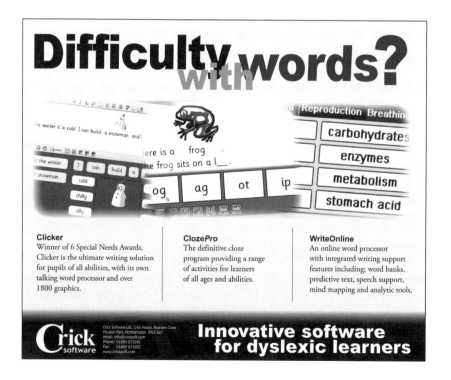

Speech, Language and Literacy – The Overlapping Difficulties

Rosie Wood

There are many reasons why a child may struggle due to speech and language problems once she, or more likely he, starts school. Most people are familiar with the problems for children with:

- English as a second language – until the child is fully accomplished in the new language needed for learning.
- Speech / language delay – until skills have caught up with those of peers
- Speech and language impairment – where there is a speech / language disorder.
- Language disadvantage – those whose environment has not given them the opportunity to learn fluent speech and language skills.
- Specific Learning Difficulties (SpLD) – for instance Dyslexia (and sometimes Dyspraxia) .

For all such children there will be some 'knock on' effects for their development in literacy. And sadly, the Matthew principle tends to apply to reading and writing and spelling.

Those who learn to read, and enjoy reading, develop vocabulary and language skills which helps them to read better, an upward spiral. But children whose spoken language skills are poor and who struggle with learning to read, find themselves in a downward spiral.

Reading requires both 'top down' (grammar and vocabulary) and bottom up (decoding and letter/sound links) skills.

"For true comprehension the reader has to do more than decode ...."

He also needs to…

"distinguish the important message, ie what the main idea is, what is relevant, and what is irrelevant."

McLean & Wood, (2004) Reading Comprehension.

And for writing:

"Speaking is the bridge between thinking and writing. Children must first be able to express their ideas in spoken language before they can express them in written language."

Reilly & Murray (2004) Thinking and Speaking in Primary Schools.

And finally, in order to be able to spell, children need phonological awareness skills so that they can listen to the sequence of sounds in a word in their 'mind's ear', segment the sound stream into its component parts and then convert those sounds into the letters used to represent them.

Many dyslexic children may have a variety of difficulties with speech and language. They are often late to talk and may have persistent speech articulation problems. Sometimes these are very noticeable, but often they may present as mumbled speech, a lack of clarity with consonant clusters (e.g. str*awberry*, spla*sh*) or missing unstressed syllables (e.g. *'puter, 'nana*). They may find it hard to perceive differences between similar sounding words (e.g. *ball/bowl, lost/lots jury/jewellery*). Retrieving words from the child's word store or lexicon can be a struggle because they cannot recall the sound pattern they need. Phonological awareness, the ability to reflect on the sound stream, to divide it into syllables, to detect and produce rhyme and to isolate individual sounds (phonemes) is often a major weakness in dyslexia, affecting both decoding in reading and encoding for spelling.

Results from studies undertaken by Stackhouse et al (2007) indicate that some groups of children are particularly at risk:

- Critical Age Hypothesis – Children who have not resolved their speech and/or language problems by ~CA 5;6 are likely to have associated literacy problems.
- Children who have speech AND language problems more likely to have literacy problems than those who have only speech OR only language problems.
- Children with speech AND language problems had more severe speech difficulties plus problems with speech input, phoneme awareness and letter knowledge.
- Children with persisting speech difficulties are likely to have associated spelling difficulties.
- There is a lasting impact of their speech and language difficulties on their educational performance (e.g. at SATS and GCSE level) even when 'resolved'.

(Stackhouse 2011 'Co-occurring Speech Input and Output Difficulties' presentation at B.D.A. Conference.)

It is clear that for children whose speech and language skills are weak, a more extensive assessment procedure is needed so that remediation may be properly focused. There is little point in teaching phonics to a child who does not have the necessary underpinning phonological awareness skills !

To be sufficiently comprehensive such an assessment will cover:

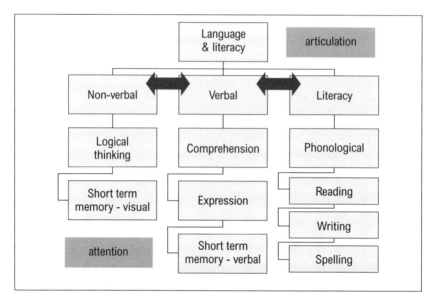

Good assessors know that test results give only limited information; their observation, analysis and cross referencing of the results provide a detailed learning profile that can lead directly to focused, effective support.

For children with more severe phonological awareness difficulties, additional analysis may be necessary. Speech and language therapists familiar with the Psycholinguistic Framework use this systematic hypothesis testing approach to assess speech processing skills as a basis for highly individualised remediation. Formal and informal tests assess a child's speech processing system at key points from ear to brain to mouth:

Basic hearing

- via speech *input* (asking detailed questions such as:. Can the child discriminate speech sounds without reference to lexical representations (e.g. auditory discrimination between non-words) ? Are his phonological representations accurate and is he aware of their structure ? (e.g. can he detect articulation errors in another ? Can he silently detect first sounds of words ?)

Lexical representations (word store in the brain which includes sound patterns, meanings, pictorial representations, associations etc)

■ via speech *output* (asking questions such as: Can he manipulate phonological units ? Can he articulate real words accurately ? Can he articulate non-words accurately ?)
Adequate sound production (which may include oral examination)

This information can then be used to reach those parts a more standard 'remediation programme' may *not* reach !

We expect very young children in school to be able to learn to read and write and spell; these are skills which depend upon spoken language. The Royal College of Speech and Language Therapists' Specific Interest Group in SpLD (RCSLT SIG in SpLD) holds regular meetings and an annual conference at which it welcomes colleagues interested in the interface between speech and language and literacy. (SIG contact: Patricia Fisher **patriciafisher@dsl.pipex.com**). Continued collaboration among teachers, parents and speech and language therapists will help us all to improve our support for children with these combined difficulties, allowing them into the world of literacy and education.

References

Snowling,M Stackhouse,J.(2006) *Dyslexia, Speech and Language: A Practitioner's Handbook.* 2nd edn. London, Wiley.

Stackhouse,J. Wells,B. (1997) *Children's Speech and Literacy Difficulties 1: A Psycholinguistic Framework.* London:Whurr.

Reilly,J. Murray,S.(2004) *Thinking and Speaking in Primary Schools.* Target Series:Barrington Stoke.

Reilly,J. Murray,S.(2004) *Listening and Understanding in Primary Schools.* Target Series:Barrington Stoke.

McLean,B. Wood,R. (2004) *Reading Accuracy*. Target
   Series:Barrington Stoke.

Visual Processing difficulties in Dyslexia

John Stein

Most people agree that many dyslexic children find difficulty with reading, because they are poor at breaking down word sounds to match with the letters that represent them; they have poor phonemic awareness. But this doesn't explain why they have this problem. Furthermore not all dyslexics do have phonological difficulties, and everyone who actually teaches dyslexics knows that a substantial proportion fail to benefit from intensive phonological training.

Visual Symptoms

Many of these children have visual problems; they complain that they cannot see the letters properly on the page because they appear to blur, move around and change their order. This disorder often gives them headaches when they try to read. Such symptoms are common after lesions of the parts of the brain responsible for controlling visual attention and eye movements, often giving rise to acquired dyslexia. Underactivity of these areas has also been implicated in developmental dyslexia. Up to two thirds of the children with delayed reading that we see in our clinics experience such visual problems.

Vision is the main sense used for reading. When we are learning to read, we have to learn to visually identify each letter or group of letters and remember their correct order, and how to translate them into the sounds they stand for. In practised readers this auditory translation is unnecessary; whole words are recognised visually and their meaning extracted directly. Nevertheless even for practised readers the essential sense is vision. If your vision is not stable it is not surprising that you find it difficult to lay down reliable memory traces of the correct spelling of words (orthography).

Magnocellular neurones

We now know that these visual processes depend greatly on the proper development of a set of large nerve cells called magnocellular neurones (M cells) that respond rapidly to visual motion. If the eyes wander off a letter being identified these signal this movement to the eye muscle servo system; this then moves the eyes back by the same amount to keep them on target. So M cells are extremely important for maintaining stable visual perception of letters, and preventing them appearing to move around or blur.

Many dyslexics have impaired development of these M nerve cells, mainly as a result of genetic vulnerability. When these neurones are examined through a microscope in dyslexic brains *post mortem* they are seen to be smaller and more disordered. Also in life, if the M cells in the eye of a dyslexic are selectively stimulated, their responses are often found to be weaker than in good readers. Imaging their activity in the brain has confirmed that these systems do not work so precisely in dyslexics. This mild magnocellular impairment leads to poorer attentional and eye fixation stability, and the resulting perceptual instability underlies these children's visual difficulties with learning to read.

Blue Filters

We have found that one simple way of improving children's ability to focus their attention and fixate their eyes accurately on the text they're trying to read is to ask them to look at it through blue filters. The peak transmission of the blue filters we use is at the wavelength of 450 nm, so they cut out most red and green light. This blue light selectively stimulates another kind of retinal cell that has recently been discovered. These feed, not into the conscious visual cortex, but into an area deep inside the brain, the hypothalamus. This contains our body clock which, as well as controlling many other daily rhythms, wakes us up in the morning and puts us to sleep at night. These rhythms need to be entrained to sunrise; hence the blue sensitive retinal cells are there to stimulate the hypothalamus to wake us earlier in summer and later in winter.

The main nerve cells switched on during such arousal are the magnocellular ones described earlier. So blue light promotes alertness, and thus our blue filters probably help dyslexics by increasing their ability to harness their M cells to better focus their attention. Not only do they help reading in susceptible children, but they also improve poor sleeping. Serendipitously we also discovered that the blue light can reduce children's migraine headaches, probably because diurnal malfunction of the cortical pain system that causes migraine, is also controlled by the hypothalamic clock.

A small number of children, particularly those with weak convergence of their eyes to look at close print, are helped more by yellow filters. These probably work in a different way. In the retina the red and green cone receptors provide the main input to magnocellular neurones. Yellow filters allow red and green, but not blue, light to pass through to the receptors; so they directly boost the output of magnocells. This is sometimes more effective than blue in relieving the children's visual symptoms.

Even though the great majority of recent research that has examined the role of the magnocellular system has confirmed that its development is mildly impaired in dyslexics, this is not accepted by everyone. Its mildness means that you need very sensitive tests to detect it. Hence some studies have failed to show the M deficit, and the whole idea remains controversial.

Identifying visual problems

It is by no means essential to accept the M theory however, to be able to help children with visual problems when reading. All visual symptoms should be taken seriously and every child with reading difficulties should be asked about them, because there are simple ways of helping. In practice one should ask four simple questions: do letters appear to blur; do they appear to move around; do they ever go double, and do you get headaches when you try to read? If the child's answer to any of these questions is yes, it is sensible to see whether looking at small print through a deep blue overlay (Kodak Wratten number 47) or, more rarely, a yellow one (no.15) reduces their visual symptoms. 2/3rds of the 7-10 year old children who attend our clinics for reading difficulties have one or more of these visual symptoms, and almost all of these can be helped to reduce them by wearing blue or yellow filters for all reading and close work. Thereafter their reading usually improves greatly.

We have tested a variety of other colours. It is often claimed that each child needs a different colour and that one should have up to 2000 colours to select from to properly treat each individual child; but we have found that blue or yellow help most of the children with visual reading symptoms whom we see. In a recent trial we found that wearing blue filters when reading could increase dyslexic children's reading age by 9 ms after 3 months wearing them, compared with only 2 months reading improvement in those receiving placebos because without help most dyslexics fall further and further behind.

We find that two thirds of children with reading difficulties can be helped with these very simple visual treatments. Reducing their visual discomfort does not necessarily improve their reading immediately however, because the improved visual input has to be transferred to more precise visual representations of words in memory and also to become correctly associated with the words' sounds. The auditory processing required for the latter can additionally be impaired in dyslexics. Nevertheless successfully treating the visual symptoms in these children usually leads to significantly improved reading and smaller improvements in spelling within 3 months, without any additional teaching help.

Teachers and Professionals

The B.D.A. Dyslexia Friendly Quality Mark

Eorann Lean

The British Dyslexia Association's mission is to create a dyslexia friendly society. To achieve this we set the standard nationally and internationally for Dyslexia Friendly practices with our Dyslexia Friendly Quality Mark. Our Quality Mark strives to address barriers throughout society. There are tailor-made criteria for the main areas that dyslexic individuals progress through in their lives: schools, colleges, vocational training establishments, universities and companies. Many organisations are already starting to show some improvements in dyslexia awareness but we believe that it is not just about having appropriate classes, seminars and meetings but about the whole of the organisation; its practices and its ethos.

The B.D.A. Dyslexia Friendly Quality Mark brings about and celebrates good practice. It leads to organisations with awareness and understanding, that identify and work hard to provide appropriately for dyslexic individuals and signpost to further information as required. Organisations that achieve the B.D.A. Dyslexia Friendly Quality Mark are making a real difference to the dyslexic individuals that are part of them. We are very proud of our B.D.A. Quality Mark organisations and provide them with our Dyslexia Friendly Quality Mark logo to highlight their achievements and signpost dyslexic individuals to them.

'if they can't learn the way we teach, can we teach the way we learn?' (Harry Chasty, circa 1980)

The majority of dyslexics will spend most of their time in school in mainstream classrooms, being taught by non-specialist tutors. So it is vital that general classroom environments are dyslexia friendly and employ appropriate teaching methods, in addition to educational establishments providing specialist teaching

programmes for one-to-one and small group intervention work. The Quality Mark is a step towards dyslexic children being able to flourish alongside their contemporaries within the education system.

The Dyslexia Friendly Qulaity Mark also reaches schools through Local Education Autorities (LEAs)/ Children's services. Sixteen LEAs/ Children's services have achieved the award which has a wide impact on many schools. Many of the LEAs have been able to go on to initiate programmes that they have adapted from the B.D.A. criteria, for schools in their area. This spreading of good practice by LEAs means many more schools can be reached.

The process for the Dyslexia Friendly Quality Mark is different for every category as they are specific to the setting, however, the basic structure is the same. So to understand this process better let us take what an individual school does. For instance, Primary School A. School A already has some good practice but has noticed that their dyslexic pupils are not reaching their potential. The self-audit which is the fist step of the Quality Mark helps them take an in-depth look at the school. The B.D.A. standards help to show them what dyslexia friendly activities they already doing well and where they can improve. School A realises that while they were working hard to provide handouts, and support for writing activities, they needed to strengthen their systems for early identification of possible dyslexic difficulties and to deliver effective intervention programs as early as possible. So they draw up an action plan to fix this which includes additional staff training in quality first dyslexia friendly teaching and support.

School A works hard for a year, and as they already had much good practice to begin with, they successfully complete their action plan. They prepare a "Record of Evidence" to show that they are now meeting each of the B.D.A. Quality Mark criteria, and submit this to the B.D.A.. The verification visit from the B.D.A. is then booked. At the verification visit the B.D.A. observes classes, interviews teachers, teaching assistants, governors, parents and pupils. One of the pupils is Freddie.

Freddie says that he has always struggled because he saw the world in pictures rather than words. But since his teacher started demonstrating what she wanted by actually doing it, Freddie could make a 'video' of the instructions and can now keep up with his peers more easily.

School A satisfies all the criteria and they are awarded the B.D.A. Dyslexia Friendly Quality Mark. They also receive a report on how they can continue to embed good practice. The B.D.A. will then come back every three years to reverify School A. The teachers have noticed the great impact that the Quality Mark has had on the school. Those children they were worried about are no longer falling behind but are coming out of their shells and showing improved literacy skills.

Of course, School A is only a created example but there is evidence that dyslexia friendly primary schools show decreasing numbers of children failing in reading at the end of primary school. Pupils report that they feel people understand their dyslexia more, staff and pupils help them more, they feel able to ask for help, and their reading and writing skills have improved. The pupils know that they are not on their own in having dyslexic difficulties and they are helped to understand their potential strengths. Teachers also report that going through the B.D.A. Dyslexia Friendly Quality Mark process doesn't only help the dyslexic pupils, but those with other special needs as well. There are many techniques for teachers through which they can adopt active, fun multisensory approaches to teaching and learning. It is not only the dyslexic pupils who enjoy and are more likely to recall the lessons.

While the Dyslexia Friendly Quality Mark is an important goal, there are other things that schools can do to help dyslexic individuals. The British Dyslexia Association is able to send trainers into schools, colleges and universities to deliver in-service training on dyslexia friendly teaching and learning environments. These INSET sessions are very well received and can be 'bespoke' according to the needs of the individual educational establishment. This is an excellent way of spreading information, which may include the key signs of dyslexia, when to refer for further assessment, the need for and nature of additional teaching provisions and in-class support, dyslexic friendly teaching for the classroom, understanding dyslexia difficulties and potential learning strengths, effective use of resources including assistive technology, dyslexia friendly classroom environments and appropriate access arrangements.

If they can't work the way you work- what is your company missing out on?

Dyslexia can be considered a disability where it is a long-standing difficulty that has a negative impact on daily living. Companies have to ensure that they comply with the Equalities Act 2010 not to discriminate against those with disabilities. The Quality Mark can be a very efficient and effective way of doing this. However, the Quality Mark offers more to companies this. Dyslexic individuals have a lot to give a company. Dyslexic individuals can show strong creativity, strategic thinking and problem solving skills. An employee who has had to work throughout their life to deal with barriers and think of new and different ways to process information to the majority of people has gained a lot of skills and resilience. Furthermore a person who thinks and see things in a different way is potentially incredibly useful to a company – they are literally thinking outside the box! Changing your work space, support, technological aids, or working practices so that their new thoughts and ideas can be expressed and flourish can only be an asset to business.

As well as the Quality Mark, the B.D.A. offers training talks in dyslexia friendly practices for companies and organisations. This is a great way to encourage companies to start to think about how to address the needs of both the organisation and the employees in an inclusive and positive way.

The Dyslexia Friendly Quality Mark is a partnership process, we want the organisations to become dyslexia friendly and we work with them to help them achieve that. The Quality Mark was created to be a mutually beneficial solution to the barriers of dyslexia. It is there to overcome these barriers so that dyslexic individuals and organisations can reach their potential.

For further information on the B.D.A. Quality Mark and related INSET/ training, please contact:

Joanne Gregory
Quality Mark Development Manager
01656-724-585
07786-071-020

e-mail: **qualitymark@bdadyslexia.org.uk**
Quality Mark details: **www.bdadyslexia.org.uk**

Synthetic Phonics

Ruth Miskin

Children who learn to read easily are more likely to read at home from choice, By nine, they could be reading over two million words a year. They love reading. They read in two days what poor readers read in one year. They also read books that contain words they wouldn't come across if they couldn't read - cacophony, diminutive, impenetrable. They are nearly always successful at school.

Poor readers are easy to spot: their eyes flit from the picture, to face, to random letter, guessing wildly. But there is another group of children who just 'get by' at school. They have a reading age of eight or nine for three years running. Reading books don't come home; reading diaries disappear and parents become niggled and bothered.

It is much easier for children in Spain, Italy, Poland, Finland or Germany. Spanish children learn 29 ways to read their 24 speech sounds with the 26 letters of the Roman alphabet. This is called a simple code: one sound- one letter; the match is pretty close. Spanish children can then read anything, albeit slowly to begin with.

But our children need to learn 150+ ways to read the 44 English speech sounds with the same 26 letters; English has the most complex code in the world, so learning the 26 sounds of the alphabet doesn't get you very far. To make it even harder, many reading schemes contain all the 150+ ways from the very beginning. It doesn't help if there is only one word on a page if you can't read it!

Some children learn to read whatever system you use, but others just don't. They spend years struggling in lessons - bored, mildly disruptive and withdrawn.

In Read Write Inc. we make learning to read as simple as we can. We pretend – just for a little while – that learning to read is as easy as learning to read Spanish.

Children learn to read and write a simple code. They learn the 44 speed sounds by picture-morphing e.g. a c-c-c-caterpillar (the same shape as c) is morphed into 'c'. As soon as they can read the first five at speed, they learn to read words in 'Fred Talk' (sound-blending).

Then, importantly, they read *lively* books with words they can *work out by sound-blending*. The books are fun, so the children will want to read them again and again. They have a good plot, so we can we talk about the story.

Once they have mastered the simple code, they learn the full code with its alternate spellings of the speech sounds.

The more sounds they learn, the more books they can read. Children who learn quickly read fewer books than those who need lots of practice. As the children learn *how* to read, we read lots of stories *to* the children and learn poems and rhymes by heart. This pattern continues until they can read the same stories we read to them, for themselves.

In the same step-by-step way, children learn to write sounds, words with the sounds they know, then simple sentences and stories. We compose stories orally, using talking prompts and partner work.

Close homogeneous grouping – just while children learn *how* to read - means that children make much greater progress. It allows children to read and write at their progress level every day for 30 minutes to one hour - not just once a week or for a couple of minutes a day. No wonder they learn so quickly. A few children, with particular needs, also receive 10 minutes one-to-one practice before the lesson, so they feel successful from the start. No-one is allowed to fall through the net.

All staff are trained by one of our trainers, so everyone knows what each other is doing; using the same methods makes a huge difference to children's progress. The trainers are both very knowledgeable and inspiring - they show teachers how to make learning to read immensely enjoyable.

Parents can easily help if they want to – there is no mystery to what we do. What's more, children learn my system so well they can even teach their younger brothers and sisters! Many schools now show the parents what to do, but if they don't, parents can download a simple guide from the Read Write Inc. website.

There are now over two thousand schools using Read Write Inc. across the world . Many are in disadvantaged areas, but increasingly more and more independent schools are adopting the system so their children can learn to read and write more quickly.

It's a simple system, but it does need to be well-led by a senior teacher who recognises that a school is only as good as the success of its most vulnerable child. It just takes enthusiasm and good organisation!

Ruth's ten top tips for teachers and parents

1. Teach 5 sound-letter/s correspondences a week, starting with single letters and then going on to the sounds represented by two or three letters (e.g. *sh, oo air, igh*). Use visual-auditory mnemonics to help children learn them quickly – e.g. d in the shape of the dinosaur, g in the shape of a girl. Review the sounds at least 5 times a day until children can read them speedily.

2. Teach letter formation alongside this, using the mnemonic phrases to help: e.g. d – "round the dinosaur's bottom up his neck and down to his feet". Teach children to sit comfortably at a table and to use a correct pencil grip.

3. Teach children to understand and to speak in 'Fred Talk' - saying words in sounds e.g. r-e-d, b-l-ue, b-a-ck, ch-ee-k.

4. Once children can read the first few sounds speedily, show them how to read words in Fred Talk and work out the word e.g. m-a-t, mat.

5. Teach children to spell words using Fred Talk. Show them how to pinch a different finger as they say each sound: e.g. mat, m-a-t.

6. Teach 'red' words for reading and spelling (common words containing an unusual spelling of a sound). Help children look for the letters that 'work' and ones that are tricky.

7. Match stories closely to the sounds they can read, so they can apply their word-reading skills independently. No guessing needed!

8. Teach alternative spellings for sounds once their word reading is confident.

9. Read lots of stories *to* children – they will soon be able to read these for themselves.

10. Put learning to read at the heart of the school and persevere with children who take longer to learn. Never give up!

www.ruthmiskinliteracy.com (training)
www.readwriteinc.com (resources)

Teaching the dyslexic child: 5 key factors

Sue Thirtle

A very wise and experienced teacher once told me that the ideas I thought were innovative were only the latest fad on the pendulum swing of how to teach children successfully. At that time, in reading for example, there were exponents of the successful use of phonics, while others poured scorn on such unfashionable methods and advocated teaching through 'real' reading books, or teaching through a topic. The Literacy Hour brought many of these methods together in the teaching of reading. It was 'OK' to use phonics alongside identifying the shape of the word, any picture cues on the page and the sense of the text. Now, the teaching of phonics as the primary method is back in vogue, but there are beginning to be tweaks around the edges. Software packages have brought another welcome dimension to this picture. For some dyslexics, using specialist computer programmes are a non-judgmental and generally peer-accepted way of being taught.

Could this child be dyslexic?

In my early years of teaching, I was amazed that some bright and articulate children in my classes could not learn to read through the latest fashionable method, while others did so with ease. It was a parent of one of these children in my class who first asked the question, 'Could my child be dyslexic?' and suddenly the reasons for the difficulties experienced by these children were clear. My journey through discovering dyslexia had begun, but the more I learnt, the more I discovered that the subject itself was very unclear.

To begin with, there is no agreed definition of dyslexia, so if identification measures cannot be agreed, it is difficult to agree teaching strategies. I have been involved in the writing of a number of guidelines for teachers and parents, which would not have been written if we had waited for a definition acceptable to everyone. Challenges between parents and schools are often around the perceptions of parents, rightly or wrongly, that the needs of their children are not being met. If a parent says there is a problem, then the school should always take this seriously because the anxiety of the parent will always impact upon the child. I cannot begin to count the number of parents who have told me that a teacher has said that their child is not dyslexic without any evidence either way.

So what are the 5 keys to teaching the dyslexic child?

1. **Facilitate a belief in their abilities, self confidence and enable success.** Actions that destroy any of these will lay the foundations for failure of any interventions, however carefully delivered. A child who cannot read and is repeatedly belittled by peers, parents, and sometimes even teachers, will become the class clown. A parent once told me of his frustration with his child who couldn't read 'the'. He said that he had told him in exasperation, "Look you read 'the' there, it's the same word, why can't you read it there!" Susan Hampshire, the actress, says that as a child, if she had broken her leg people would have been more sympathetic, but her dyslexia was a hidden handicap that was not understood. In your class or tutor group there will be at least three or four dyslexics on a continuum from mild to severe. Just one bad experience can sour self-belief for life. How many people do you know who 'can't do maths'?

2. **Teach the way children learn, not the way you prefer to teach.** All teachers have preferred teaching styles and often find it hard to understand that, if their usually successful methods do not work, it might just be the problem of the intervention programme, rather than the fault of the child. I have heard a number of teachers say in all seriousness that a child has been 'doing' the same phonic programme for years, but still has not learnt their initial sounds. The joy of teaching dyslexics is that there is always something that will capture their interest to begin the learning process and the role of the teacher is to find the teaching method to ignite the spark.

3. **Use a tried and tested teaching programme which can demonstrate progress can be made.** Many teachers continue teaching their dyslexic pupils effectively despite new initiatives. Inspectors once told one of my colleagues that she must stop teaching reading through phonics, and teach through using 'interesting' books. There was no thought given to the fact that she successfully, regularly, taught every child in her class to read. If a teaching method is producing both quantifiable and qualitative results, then the only reason for change would be for those children for whom it is not working.

    Greg Brooks reports on a range of interventions in his third edition of research (2007) in *What Works for Children with Literacy Difficulties?*

    http://tinyurl.com/66cgwsm

    One unsurprising conclusion of his research is that:
    '*Ordinary teaching ('no intervention') does not enable children with literacy difficulties to catch up.*' (2.16)

4. **Have high expectations.** The Progression Guidance is becoming more and more used in schools **http://tinyurl.com/44n6ba3**. This states:

    One of the key principles is for there to be high expectations for all learners identified as having SEND.

The progression measures set out a clear national expectation of the minimum rate of progress that all pupils of all abilities should make: **two National Curriculum levels of progress between Key Stage 1 and Key Stage 2 and three National Curriculum levels of progress between Key Stage 2 and Key Stage 4. (3,3)**

Teaching interventions are often better in short intensive bursts rather than years of repeats of the same programme. These programmes should be assessed for effectiveness over short periods of time. If they don't work, they should be changed. This guidance is very helpful and expectations for dyslexics and all children with Special Educational Needs and Disabilities (SEND) should be high.

5. **Use a systematic, structured and regularly evaluated support programme overseen or carried out by an experienced teacher, preferably with specialist knowledge.** Some schools, especially secondary, find it hard to fit specialist teaching of dyslexics into the way lessons are timetabled. Teaching assistant support is usually deployed to support dyslexics to access the curriculum, rather than to address their underlying difficulties. As Greg Brooks (see above) suggests:

   Although good classroom teaching is the bedrock of effective practice, most research suggests that children falling behind their peers need more help than the classroom normally provides. This help requires coordinated effort and training. (2.16)

In some schools the children needing the most support are being taught by teaching assistants. Very often they have been trained to deliver a particular intervention and whether appropriate or not, that is what the children will receive, whether dyslexic or having difficulties with learning for other reasons. These interventions are rarely monitored for effectiveness.

A whole-school approach

A more powerful support for dyslexics and for all children with learning difficulties is the Dyslexia Friendly School initiative supported by the British Dyslexia Association. **http://tinyurl.com/3old84k** Schools achieving this award have trained their whole staff, including non-teaching staff, and have standards to fulfil over time. This can be hugely successful and ensures that everyone understands the issues around teaching the dyslexic child.

Bredon School

Pull Court, Bushley, Tewkesbury, Gloucestershire. GL20 6AH

Telephone: +44 (0) 1684 293156 Fax: +44 (0)1684 276392
Email: enquiries@bredonschool.co.uk www.bredonschool.org

B.D.A. Accreditation for Dyslexia Specialist Teachers

Mike Johnson

At the start of his second report, "Identifying and Teaching Children and Young People with Dyslexia and Literacy Difficulties" (Rose, J, 2009) Sir Jim Rose makes the following statements:

> "Reading disorders have been extensively researched such that dyslexia, the existence of which was once questioned, is now widely recognised as a specific difficulty in learning to read. Research also shows that dyslexia may affect more than the ability to read and write. (p.2)
>
> Secondly, the long running debate about its existence should give way to building professional expertise in identifying dyslexia and developing effective ways to help learners overcome its effects. (p.9)"

February this year saw the 25th anniversary of the earliest awards of Associate Membership of the British Dyslexia Association (AMBDA) given in 1986 following courses provided by the then Dyslexia Institute and the Helen Arkell Dyslexia Centre. Courses leading to the awards of Approved Teacher Status (ATS) and AMBDA are now seen as the 'Gold Standard' for developing such specialist professional expertise. Around 2,500 places on ATS and AMBDA courses were fully funded by the Teacher Development Agency in 2010-11 and holders of AMBDA are eligible to apply for award of an Assessment Practising Certificate, allowing its holders to perform formal assessments for Dyslexia/Specific Learning Difficulties (SpLD) and subsequent concessions, previously the province of only educational psychologists. The only trained teacher needed for the new 'Free Schools' is one with a specialist qualification for the teaching of pupils with SEN. A course leading to AMBDA would seem most appropriate. We have come a long way in 25 years.

The B.D.A. now has a full set of awards offering a complete career progression for educational professionals working with pupils having difficulties with literacy. For Teaching Assistants this progression begins with Accredited Learning Support Assistant (ALSA). This is normally offered by a Local Authority with support and validation from a college or university. It focuses on working with teachers with understanding and practical skills. It can be followed by entry to the new Approved Practitioner Status (APS) award. The criteria for this award are the same as for Approved Teacher Status (ATS) and courses are co-taught but APS is awarded to those without UK qualified teacher status (QTS). This is particularly important given the significant proportion of pupils with SEN being supported by teaching assistants and support assistants now have a clear specialist career progression.

ATS is recognised by the Teacher Development Agency (TDA) as the basic qualification for a specialist dyslexia/SpLD teacher. Those holding the award (and APS) have a critical understanding of the nature and causes of dyslexia and are competent in both informal, curriculum-based assessment and the delivery of appropriate specialist teaching.

The final award is AMB.D.A. for which QTS (or certain other professional qualifications) is an essential pre-requisite. Holders of AMBDA have a deep, critical understanding of the theories and research underpinning contemporary understanding of the nature, causes and effects of dyslexia and its assessment, They are competent in the use of both informal and psychometrically based tests and can apply for a Dyslexia/SpLD Assessment Practising Certificate enabling them to undertake formal assessment of and reporting on learners thought to have dyslexic type difficulties. Both ATS and AMBDA have specialist variations for those working in further or higher education.

In addition the B.D.A. also accredits **AMBDA Numeracy, a course** designed for those working with dyslexic learners in the mathematics classroom.

B.D.A. accredited courses must be validated by Higher Education Institutions to ensure that the highest possible standards are maintained. Full details are on the B.D.A. web site **http://www.bdadyslexia.org.uk**

Through an appointed Liaison Team courses leading to a B.D.A. award are scrutinised by the Accreditation Board composed of a balance of Course Leaders, Local Authority Representatives, Academics and Researchers from the field of dyslexia.

Increasingly in recent years the Board has been receiving proposals from outside the UK. There are currently courses in Greece, Malta and Kuwait. The latest proposals are from South Africa and Singapore. These courses fulfil the same criteria as those in the UK but also demonstrate how they take into consideration the cultural and linguistic context in which they are delivered. The Kuwait and Singapore courses are currently considering delivery in the 'home' language. In response to this increasing demand, the B.D.A. has recently launched an International Accreditation Board.

B.D.A. courses emphasise *critical* understanding of the causes and manifestations of dyslexia and of the principles underlying methods proposed for specialist intervention. B.D.A. awards require course participants to demonstrate the ability to deliver and monitor structured, sequential, phonics-based multi-sensory teaching methods. For ATS / APS and AMBDA they must also demonstrate an ability to assess learners felt to be demonstrating dyslexic type difficulties. An understanding of dyslexia friendly classroom teaching methods and the effects of dyslexia that go beyond difficulty with literacy skills is also required. The B.D.A. recognises that there are several schemes and methods that lay more emphasis in one or more of these areas and that multi-sensory instruction does not help all learners with dyslexic type difficulties. However, they feel that it is important for specialist teachers to have a firm, confident basis to begin their specialist teaching and on which to consider critically alternative methods. Similarly, the Board is not dogmatic about the way in which courses develop their courses to meet the criteria. The two members of the Board who comprise a course Liaison Team see their role as a collaborative one as 'critical friends' in the development of a course that meets the relevant criteria.

B.D.A. awards require their holders to submit a Continuing Professional Development (CPD) Portfolio every three years detailing the Professional Development Activities and direct teaching they have undertaken so as to remain conversant with knowledge, skills and professional competence required of them in their specialist teaching role.

The usual route to a B.D.A. award is through an accredited course. However, it is possible to seek accreditation through Individual Merit by presenting evidence of an ability to fulfil both the course content criteria and successful teaching of appropriate learners using structured, sequential, phonics-based multi-sensory methods.

At the heart of the accreditation of both individuals and courses lies the Accreditation Board. This meets three times a year and its members scrutinise all proposals for accreditation and four-yearly re-accreditation of courses, all requests for accreditation by individuals and all CPD Portfolios. They also consider the impact of any relevant developments in the field in relation to course content and criteria particularly that resulting from the work of the Liaison Teams. To say the meetings are lively is an understatement.

The latest developments are firstly the recognition of the B.D.A. by the SpLD Assessment Standards Committee (SASC) as one of the three awarding bodies for the SpLD Assessment Practising Certificate. Schools, colleges and parents will now no longer have to seek the services of an educational psychologist to determine the appropriate specialist intervention for a learner thought to have dyslexia. They can do this either by fulfilling the Rose recommendation that:

> *"Schools should ensure either that at least one of their teachers has, or obtains this level of expertise (ATS for informal, curriculum-based assessment, AMBDA for formal reporting)*
>
> *or*
>
> *that they have good access to such a teacher through partnership arrangements with other schools." (page 18)*

The B.D.A. Accreditation Board will continue the important work of setting and maintaining the gold standard for dyslexia/SpLD teaching and assessment training and qualifications.

Secondly:

> *"The DCSF should ask the Training Development Agency for Schools and the initial teacher training sector to build on initiatives for strengthening coverage of special educational needs and disability (including dyslexia) in initial teacher training courses."*

The B.D.A. has been proactive in this regard. At the Manchester Metropolitan University (MMU) the ITT course offers, students the ability to gain the award of ATS (ITT) through the Optional Course structure in Years 3 and 4. Following submission of evidence of appropriate professional development in their first two years of teaching this can be converted to 'full' ATS and, following an appropriate in-service course, AMBDA. All universities offering ITT will be circulated with the details of criteria leading to ATS (ITT) in the Autumn and offered support to incorporate this opportunity for their students from the member of the Accreditation Board from MMU.

It has been said that one should never make predictions, particularly about the future. However, we are clear during the next 25 years the B.D.A. will continue to strive to ensure that any learner with dyslexia will have access to an appropriately qualified specialist teacher as soon as possible.

The Role of the B.D.A. Helpline

Sue Flohr

The B.D.A. runs the only free, national dyslexia helpline in the U.K., welcoming enquiries from all individuals and organisations: parents, students, teachers, adults, employers, professionals and any organisational body.

Imagine any query, scenario or problem, even tenuously connected to dyslexia and specific learning difficulties, and you will begin to appreciate the level of knowledge, concentration and flexibility required on the B.D.A. Helpline. From parents worried about the possibility of dyslexia in their unborn child to elderly people saddened by the difficulties they have battled with all their life – and everything and everybody in between – the B.D.A. Helpline has heard it all. And even then we are surprised by the new and unexpected.

Currently the Helpline answers around 12,000 calls and 4,000 emails in a year. Approximately half of these calls come from parents with educational issues, but increasing numbers are from adults (or their partners and family members), relating to employment , discrimination, tests and exams, help with passing the driving test, issues in the judicial system, coping with life in general. Employers regularly call for advice on dyslexia assessments, reasonable adjustments such as assistive IT and the presentation of written material in a dyslexia friendly way.

The last year has seen four showings of the excellent BBC TV documentary 'Don't Call Me Stupid', featuring actress Kara Tointon and her journey with dyslexia. The first two showings over the winter, and a third in the spring, caused the Helpline to be completely overloaded with enquiries. These were not just from adults, but also parents for whom the programme rang so many bells in relation to their child's difficulties in school.

The most common queries resulting from this programme were: where could adults get a dyslexia assessment, and where could they get coloured glasses like Kara's? Unfortunately, this otherwise superb programme failed to communicate that dyslexia assessments are not funded by the NHS, and that coloured glasses are not a magic wand for reading: under 40% of people with dyslexia experience the visual stress difficulties which can be mitigated by treatment such as coloured filters. Nor is this aspect of visual treatment available under the NHS, even for children (a fact which causes much anger among some parents contacting the Helpline).

The B.D.A. has a network of 60 affiliated Local Dyslexia Associations round the country, to whom the Helpline can refer callers for local information, advice and support. To assist this process, over the past two years the Helpline has run workshops for Local Association helpliners.

So who mans the B.D.A. Helpline? The Helpline is staffed by a highly experienced full-time Helpline Manager with considerable expertise in the areas of education, further and higher education, student queries and examination access arrangement issues. Three half-time Helpline Supervisors offer further expertise in different areas, including an AMBDA SpLD trained teacher and an employment and discrimination specialist.

As parents, two Supervisors have also had experience at the sharp end of the statementing process. The staff are supported by a team of 15 volunteers, mainly working a half-day per week. Many of these have worked on the Helpline for a considerable number of years. Any query which they do not feel qualified to deal with is transferred to a Supervisor or the Manager. Regular training sessions throughout the year aim to keep everyone abreast of new information and developments, and to reinforce good practice in dealing with calls.

The Helpline aims to provide impartial information and advice, and although not trained in counselling, some long calls from distressed adults and parents can require a caring and a sympathetic response. The relationship between dyslexia and stress is daily witnessed by the team.

The B.D.A. website is a useful information resource to which callers can be directed under the section 'About Dyslexia'. In recent months, the Helpline has assembled a subsection dealing with the more common queries, under Frequently Asked Questions. We believe that this is already providing helpful answers for people, and many contacting the Helpline are able to ask more informed questions as a result of their website research. As internet use becomes ever more widespread, there may be a trend towards fewer of the more routine Helpline enquiries, leaving the more difficult and complicated issues for Helpline to deal with in the future.

Helpline staff have a good knowledge of assistive IT, but are fortunate in being able to direct technical queries to the B.D.A. New Technologies Committee for specialist help. In the fast moving technological developments of smart phones and apps, this resource is invaluable.

As a result of daily interaction with the public, the Helpline is particularly well placed to identify trends and policy issues that ought to be pursued by the B.D.A. and other organisations. In education, poor dyslexia awareness continues to be a perennial problem, as is the lack of early identification and appropriate intervention remains a problem. Continuing and new discriminatory practices in examinations is another widespread area of concern at school, apprenticeship, university, medical school and professional levels.

In employment, low levels of dyslexia awareness and understanding can create an unsympathetic working culture. The Helpline has noticed that it is often the large organisations, particularly those in the public sector, such as the NHS, who seem to have much to achieve in this area. The Helpline can refer to the B.D.A. Training Department, who offer an excellent service for employers.

B.D.A. Helpline: tel. 0845-251-9002; email: **helpline@bdadyslexia.org.uk**

The B.D.A. Helpline is accredited by the Telephone Helplines Association.

B.D.A. New Technologies Committee: **www.bdatech.org**

Dyslexia and Multilingualism

The Big Lottery Dyslexia and Multilingualism Project

Tilly Mortimore

Increasing numbers of primary age children have a first language other than English. Over 300 languages are spoken in the UK and linguistic communities vary across schools, but the education system does not offer bilingual education programmes and there are political dimensions to how bilingual learners are perceived and catered for in schools. Ofsted has identified underachievement of Black and Minority Ethnic students as a cause for concern (2003) and,while 10% of all children may be predisposed to SpLD/dyslexia, bilingual learners with English as a second language are under-representedinSpLD/Dyslexia programmes and constitute a potentially overlooked vulnerable group.

This project linked the domains of dyslexia and bilingual education to explore ways of identifying and supporting bilingual learners at risk of SpLD/dyslexia. To inform the development of CPD training and promote multilingualism and dyslexia awareness, the project has involved 55 schools across England in:

- trialling and evaluating ways of identifying (screening) bilingual children for risk of SpLD/Dyslexia;

- providing assessment and support materials for bilingual and dyslexic learners

- training SENCos and TAs in their use;

A review of literature was undertaken prior to developing design, materials and practical strategies. This article provides a brief overview of emerging issues: the nature of the bilingual learner; the impact of bilingualism upon literacy acquisition; implications for SpLD/dyslexia identification and assessment procedures and support.

Being Bilingual– linguistic and cultural diversity

Being bilingual means having access to / using two+ languages on a daily basis, rather than learning a foreign language. A 'bilingual' child is not necessarily fully fluent in each language across varied oral and literate domains and purposes. Thus, different children within school may be operating at varying levels in two or more languages. Research suggests a reciprocal relationship between the development and use of the first and second language. The extent to which the classroom acknowledges the cultural identity and L1 alongside the additional language, English, will affect a child's development. The closer the child is to full competence in two languages, the more likely they are to obtain cognitive advantages (Baker, 2006).

Motivation, previous educational practices, linguistic and cultural backgrounds, alongside opportunities and support from home and school will influence individual acquisition of spoken and written language. Bilingual proficiency may develop if both first language (L1) and English are seen positively by the learner and have high status in school, family and community. The result will be 'additive bilingualism' ,where L1 proficiency enhances English acquisition and offers cognitive and social advantages. Many English schools, however, exhibit a more 'subtractive' context - privileging English and implying L1 is unimportant or even disadvantages learning. This can undermine self-esteem and L1 proficiency, potentially resulting in lower cognitive development and poorer achievement in English.

A child's culture influences every aspect of cognitive skills and aptitudes (Rogoff, 2005). Hence, any explanation of literacy difficulties must incorporate not only individual children's stories, but their culturally diverse, multi-lingual communities (Cummins 2000) and recognise that difficulties may arise from school and teaching approaches rather than from within the children or their attempts to acquire literacy in English. Hence assessing bilingual children is complex and needs to be considered within the context of such issues as cultural and linguistic backgrounds and previous educational experiences, as well as children's social and emotional development.

Acquiring Literacy

In addition to the impact of socio-cultural differences upon the development of cognitive skills, different ways of communicating and forms of language promote different cognitive skills.

Reading in any language rearranges the length and breadth of the brain…. there are multiple pathways to fluent comprehension, with a continuum of efficiency taking varied forms among the varied writing systems. (Wolf, 2008, p. 64)

Hence the importance of knowing if a child is literate in L1. 43 languages were spoken by project children. These languages may be logographic, syllabalic, alphabetic or phonemic. Some are transparent with regular phoneme-grapheme mapping; English is opaque, comparatively unpredictable and arguably the most challenging. With a few exceptions, research comparing the development of reading across international languages focuses on European languages, but even these languages exhibit variation.

Seymour (2005) suggests that all conventionally developing readers pass through similar stages, but speed of progress and development of cognitive structures is influenced by the phonology, morphology and orthography of the spoken language – progressing more swiftly in transparent languages. Some bilingual learners may therefore struggle more in one language than the other, although strengths and weaknesses in phonology, memory and fluency experienced in L1 transfer to L2. (Ziegler et al, 2005).

What are the implications for identifying SpLD/ dyslexia?

Phonological processing is universally implicated in literacy acquisition (Everatt et al, 2010); learning to read in a transparent language may enhance phonological skills (Van Oorden&Kloos, 2005). The Rose Review (2009) identified deficits in phonological processing, verbal memory and verbal processing speed as indicative of SpLD/dyslexia. Will these be triggers across all languages? The focus and structure of the language will affect the difficulties identified (Wolf, 2008) so learners of a transparent language may struggle tobecome fluent, phonological problems will occur in opaque languages, whilevisuo-spatial memory issues arise with non-alphabetic scripts. Although the 'standard' phonological deficit remains a marker, it may not be so easy to spot in a bilingual child who is already literate in a transparent L1.

Assessing bilingual pupils is complex and must be placed within thechild's cultural and linguistic background, previous educational experiences and social and emotional development. The following information is essential: knowledge of the child's culture, current and previous educational experience, reading history and the characteristics of L1 with implications for dyslexic markers in the language. A full assessment would cover literacy skills plus underlying abilities in:

- listening comprehension,
- phonological awareness/processing;
- auditory memory and discrimination;
- visual processing – copying and memory;
- verbal and non-verbal reasoning;
- rapid naming:
- writing skills.

Ideally, some test materials in L1 should explore skills in L1. Rapid naming emerges as a clear indicator and a potential area for devising L1 tasks.

A culture-fair assessment must, however, avoid the damaging impact of false positive or negative labellingbased on prioritizingpotentially misleadingwithin-child assessment measures. The practical purpose for assessment must be justified. An assessor must be sensitive to the implications of learning differences or 'labelling' a child within the family's culture. Providing a profile of strengths and weaknesses to inform support may be preferable. Reportsmust be accessible for parents, regardless of knowledge of English.

Structuring support

The review suggested that support shouldbe structured, reinforced, cumulative and multi-sensory, incorporating strategies to:

- improve phonological processing skills (including verbal memory), oral language development and explicit vocabulary teaching and work with morphemes;
- develop comprehension skills (such as reciprocal reading);
- improve memory and processing speed;
- consider cultural background and experiences, structure of L1, and learners' attitude to literacy.

Conclusions

Multi-sensory structured practice for students with SpLD/ dyslexia should be enhanced with careful exploration of the individual child's story, cultural context and literacy history and enriched with explicit language development. The complexity emerging from the literature,alongside the richly varied experiences of the project children, counsels caution in data interpretation, raising questions about the implications of identifying risk of dyslexia and the nature of support.

Baker C (2006) *Foundations of Bilingual Education and Bilingualism* (4th edition) .Clevedon: Multilingual Matters

Cummins J (2000) *Language. Power and Pedagogy: Bilingual Children in the Crossfire* (series title: Bilingual Education and Bilingualism), Clevedon: Multilingual Matters

Everatt, J, Ocampo, D, Kazuvire, V, Styliani, N, Smythe, I, al Mannai, H, Elbeheri, G

(2010) Dyslexia in Bi-scriptal readers. In N. Brunswick, S McDougall & P de Mornay Davies (2010)(Eds), *The role of orthographies in reading and spelling*. Hove: Psychology Press

Rogoff, B (2003) *The Cultural Nature of Human Development* Oxford University Press

Rose,SJ (2009) Identifying and Teaching Children and Young People with Dyslexia and Literacy Difficulties: An independent report. **www.education.gov.uk/publications/acc 12.09.2011**

Seymour P.H.K (2005) Early Reading Development in European Orthographies in M. J. Snowling & C. Hulme (eds) The Science of *Reading. A Handbook*. 296-316 Oxford: Blackwell

Ziegler, J C, & Goswami, U C (2005). Reading acquisition, developmental dyslexia and skilled reading across languages: A psycholinguistic grain size theory. *Psychological Bulletin, 131(1), 3-29.[pdf]*

Van Orden, G C&Kloos, H (2005) Role of Phonology in Skilled Reading in M J Snowling& CHulme (eds) The Science of Reading. A Handbook. Oxford: Blackwell

Wolf, M (2008)*Proust and the Squid. The story and science of the reading brain*. Cambridge: Icon Books

The Dyslexia and Multilingualism team

B.D.A.: Kate Saunders, Liz Horobin, Jill Fernando

Bath Spa University: Anny Northcote, Mim Hutchings, Lynda Hansen, Carrie Ansell

Canterbury Christ Church University, New Zealand: Consultant: John Everatt

Dyslexia and Multilingualism: implications for teaching

Liz Horobin – British Dyslexia Association

To speak of bilingual English as an additional language (EAL) learners in schools in the UK as one single group is misleading; this seemingly straightforward label encompasses numerous variations. There are those pupils both of whose parents speak English as an additional language; those who have an English first language parent; those who have been in the UK since birth or early childhood and those who have arrived in the UK at a later age with no prior knowledge of English.

There are also those students who arrive to study in the UK having previously learned English as an additional academic language in their home country. Some learners come from home countries in which dyslexia is recognised, while others are from backgrounds where dyslexia is either unknown or regarded as a stigma. Additionally, learners may be simultaneous or sequential bilinguals; they may or may not be literate in their first language (L1); they may have learned an L1 which is alphabetic or syllabic or logographic.

Such features have a major effect on language development and should, therefore, be the starting point for any assessment of the needs of EAL learners. This is particularly important as many of the language and learning difficulties exhibited by dyslexic children will also present in children learning EAL. Children who have had limited exposure to the English language may have problems with the sounds of English and thus may appear to have weak phonological processing skills – this may be particularly true in the case of older children or those whose first language has a very different sound palate from that of English. Conversely, phonological processing difficulties may be masked by the effects of acquiring literacy in a transparent language.

Thus, it may be wise to regard any seeming difficulty with phonological processing as a potential risk indicator for dyslexia. Limited opportunities to acquire vocabulary lead to poor reading comprehension and a tendency to guess unfamiliar words; hence they often confuse those which are visually similar. A non-alphabetic L1 may mean that a pupil has not learned phonic decoding skills; a more transparent and regular mother tongue may result in problems in English with decoding complex or irregular words; while lack of experience in reading in L1 will mean that a learner has no prior skills which can be transferred to reading in L2.

These problems are compounded by the complexity of English. As Goswami puts it:

> Children who are learning to read in English need to develop multiple strategies in parallel if they are to become successful readers. They need to develop whole-word recognition strategies so they can read words like *choir* and *yacht*; they need to develop rhyme analogy strategies so that they can read irregular words like *light*, *night* and *fight*; and they need to develop grapheme-phoneme recoding strategies so that they can read regular words like *tip*, *fat*, and *dog*.
> (Goswami, 2010)

Goswami also points out that the complexity of syllable structure in the English language- its 'grain size' - can create problems for the bilingual learner grappling with identifying syllables or breaking a syllable down into its constituent phonemes.

The Big Lottery funded study, Dyslexia and Multilingualism (Mortimore et al, pending), conducted by the B.D.A. in collaboration with Bath Spa University, has focussed on identifying bilingual EAL children at risk of dyslexia at Key Stage 2 (years 4 – 6) and providing an intervention programme to help them overcome their difficulties with literacy. The intervention was structured as a daily 30 minute intervention programme delivered by teaching assistants in groups of 2:1 and focussing on reading sub-skills such as decoding, morphological awareness, knowledge of vocabulary, and comprehension, in addition to spelling.

Although the findings of this study have yet to be examined in detail, the following implications for teachers are suggested:

Screening and identification

In the initial screening process, the study used Lucid LASS Junior (8-11) plus the verbal reasoning subtest from Lucid Ability combined with the Working Memory Rating Scale (Alloway et al, 2008) and a dyslexia checklist. The accuracy of results from the screening was checked by conducting full dyslexia assessments with a subgroup of fifty pupils. Findings suggest that normal screening tools may be insufficient to identify dyslexia in bilingual EAL pupils particularly because, as suggested above, the profile presented by bilingual children may share features with the dyslexic profile, even when dyslexia is not present.

However, if it is unwise to diagnose dyslexia just on the basis of a screener, it remains the case that screening can provide teachers with a profile of strengths and weaknesses which may be useful in developing an individual learning plan for each pupil. Similarly, tests which were used to measure the progress of children involved in the project (the York Assessment of Reading Comprehension, the British Picture Vocabulary Scale, and the Wide Range Achievement Test) were able to provide valuable insights into the literacy difficulties experienced by the pupils. A comparison of scores in reading accuracy, fluency, and comprehension combined with measures of vocabulary knowledge can be particularly useful in indicating the root causes of literacy problems, helping teachers to identify which sub-skills to target.

Vocabulary

There is a high risk of assuming too great a knowledge and understanding of vocabulary in EAL pupils, whose ability to communicate verbally or to decode fluently when reading may conceal an underlying lack of comprehension. The majority of

children identified to take part in the Dyslexia and Multilingualism project had extremely poor scores in vocabulary knowledge as measured by the BPVS, something which frequently came as a surprise to their teachers. Children whose basic interpersonal communication skills appear adequate may be assumed to have a greater understanding of language than is actually the case, and this may lead to the neglect of one of their most crucial needs, namely the building of vocabulary.

Similarly, in older learners, strong verbal communication skills and an ability to recognise familiar vocabulary may conceal a lack of basic decoding skills and an inability to deal with unfamiliar words.

Spelling

Children who took part in the project used *Nessy* (Net Educational Systems Ltd) to work on their awareness of spelling rules and patterns. The competitive game playing element of this programme proved extremely successful in motivating boys and girls alike, and, coupled with multi-sensory teaching methods and over-learning, was effective in increasing children's confidence in their spelling skills.

It is likely that older learners who have missed the early years of education in the UK will also benefit from explicit teaching of phoneme/grapheme correspondence and spelling rules, as it cannot be assumed that these skills will have been taught in the pupil's home country. This is particularly true when the mother tongue is non-alphabetic. Schools in which phonics instruction is restricted to the early years may have to provide remedial instruction for older EAL children in order to ensure that the building blocks of decoding are established, and teachers should also be aware that the morphological structure of English will need to be taught explicitly.

Reading

To develop reading skills, the project used *Rapid Reading* (Pearson Heinemann), a programme which has been designed to be both dyslexia friendly and motivating, especially for boys. Key to the reading programme was the element of discussion, both of ideas in the text and of the language used, and this was crucial to building the language skills of the participating children. The programme also includes an innovative software programme, the *Rapid Reading Assistant* (RRA), which enables the pupil to either listen to the text or to read and record their own voice. The RRA was found, for a number of pupils, to greatly improve their accuracy of pronunciation. The presentation and content of the books was found to increase children's enthusiasm for reading and to succeed in building their confidence.

The growing number of bilingual EAL students studying at all levels of education in the UK has led to an increased demand from teachers for support strategies. There is concern in schools about the most appropriate ways to deal with literacy under-achievement in this group of learners and confusion over when and how to suggest that a bilingual child may be at risk of dyslexia.

While this area of research is still developing, one thing is clear: that leaving a pupil to struggle with 'acquiring' language and building vocabulary knowledge and literacy skills without additional support is not viable. Feedback from teachers and teaching assistants involved in the Dyslexia and Multilingualism project has been overwhelmingly positive and suggests that the provision of regular structured support sessions can enable bilingual learners to thrive and to reach their true potential.

References

Alloway, T.P., Gathercole, S.E. and Kirkwood, H.J. (2008) *Working Memory Rating Scale.* Pearson.

Dunn, L.M., Dunn, D.M, and National foundation for Educational Research (2009) *The British Picture Vocabulary Scale.* 3rd ed. London: GL Assessment

Goswami, U. (2010) A psycholinguistic grain size view of reading acquisition across languages. In Brunswick, N., McDougall, S. and de Mornay Davies, P. (eds) *Reading and Dyslexia in Different Orthographies* (23-42). Hove: Psychology Press.

Mortimore, T., Northcote, A., Hansen, L., Hutchings, M., Ansell, C., Saunders, K., Horobin, L., Fernando, J., & Everatt, J. (2011) *Dyslexia and Multilingualism: Evaluating the impact of a structured literacy programme*. Paper presented at BERA: Institute of Education, London

Nessy (2010) Net Educational Systems Ltd.

Rapid Reading (2007) Pearson Heinemann.

Snowling, M.J., Stothard, S.E., Clarke, P., Bowyer-Crane, C., Harrington, A., Truelove, E, Nation, K. And Hulme, C. (2009) *York Assessment of Reading for Comprehension: Passage Reading*. London: GL Assessment

Wilkinson, G.S. and Robertson, G.J. (2006) *Wide Range Achievement Test 4*. Lutz, Florida: Par

The Dyslexia and Multilingualism team

B.D.A.: Kate Saunders, Jill Fernando, Liz Horobin

Bath Spa University: Tilly Mortimore, Anny Northcote, Mim Hutchings, Lynda Hansen, Carrie Ansell.

Canterbury Christ Church University, New Zealand: Consultant: John Everatt

Dyslexia, Music and Creativity

Dyslexia and Music

Karen Marshall

As a result of consistent pressure over many years, dyslexics are receiving more support and recognition for the positive qualities they contribute in both the learning and working environments. Although these qualities vary between individuals, generally there is beginning to be an appreciation of the lateral thinking and novel approaches dyslexics often bring to problem solving. Indeed those of us who have supported dyslexics over many years are frequently amazed and humbled by some of the ideas, structures and patterns dyslexics construct in order to help them solve their own problems. When they confide a problem, it is always worth asking the individual what sort of thing they think would help them and, on occasion, offering to learn alongside them. The 'teacher' is often left wide-eyed when told of the novel way a particular individual learns.

The learning process is often a shared activity and the dyslexic learns by the very activity of the joint problem-solving progress by both the dyslexic and the non-dyslexic together. Following 10 years of working as a Learning Support Tutor at University level supporting students of differing disciplines, together with a much longer period as a class music teacher and individual instrumental teacher, the writer has reflectively concluded that it is consistent systematic and cumulative reiteration and constructive forward movement in the learning process which actually not just achieves the immediate goal sought, but also trains the dyslexic in learning how to overcome the problems associated with their particular pattern of dyslexia.

Indeed the learning of the process by which the dyslexic can learn and progress is essential if their individual talent is to be realised. It is this scaffold which permits their creativity to be set free. They need to feel free to risk experimenting and try things out and may be unable to do this without the safety net of a remembered process of learning. In the early stages of this activity, the dyslexic still needs considerable support as sometimes they get in a tangle and lose sight of the wood for the trees. They sometimes get on a sort of roller coaster and either go round in circles, or else move from one aspect to another without ever reaching a conclusion. In other words, they need to be helped to both allow their creativity to have a free rein, but also to be able to present it in some sort of convergent form. Although it can be difficult for the supporter to travel with the dyslexic and allow them to make their own mistakes, this is an essential part of the process of their learning how to handle themselves. It is extraordinarily rewarding when the supporter is told by their student that something is irrelevant or off target and then watch them delete some of the work they had spent so much time in producing.

Howard Gardner (1987), in expounding his theory of Multiple Intelligences, speaks of Music as being a comprehensive discipline because it employs all the domains of learning. Music therefore can be an ideal medium for the process described above, because it always aims for and requires an end product and does not appear to target a problem area for the dyslexic. Rather it becomes necessary for the problem to be conquered in order to achieve the end result sought.

However it may be that it is Music itself that is the vehicle for the creativity of the individual dyslexic rather than the process of learning it; musical performance or composing may be 'their thing'. The qualities it engenders and exercises are persistence, repetition, the learning of technique, kinaesthetic processes, multi-sensory activity, co-ordination, relationships between different aspects of the subject, self-expression, sheer enjoyment in exercising newly learned skills, the discovering of the real content and statement of the composer and finally the making of their own music within the conventions needed to present a satisfactory product which is also a vehicle for self expression.

Where the music student finds personal self expression in Performance rather than Composing, there is also an enormous amount of sheer hard work. Although a sensitive and inventive teacher can offer ways to help learn, there are no short cuts for anybody, dyslexic or non-dyslexic, in achieving a musical performance. The skills have to be so secure that the performer is free to 'make music' - to make the music their own as they perform. This is the gift they can then share with the listener – individuality. They give themselves in performing. It is a combination of acquired skills and their own creativity and it does not occur by accident nor without diligent attention to detail. It is as if the performer and the composer become one in making music which belongs to each of them and is shared with the listener. A non-dyslexic can reach the same goal, but by a different route. The writer and musical performer is still thrilled and amazed by the sheer joy of music and the privilege of sharing it with others, where dyslexia is merely another aspect of individuality.

For the would-be composer, it is also necessary to become familiar with the technology needed to support their self-expression. The interaction with the technology may enhance the learning process and individual creativity and it is appropriate that the teacher uses interactive technological spaces with and for the benefit of the student – once again in supporting the learning of the scaffold required.

The combination of both achieving the immediate goal, together with the memory of the training in overcoming their particular pattern of dyslexia which had previously impeded learning and/ or the presentation of a product, can become the springboard for further creativity and enterprise by the individual dyslexic. In other words they learn to 'fly on their own'. In the course of this free flight, they occasionally hit a problem for which they need help. Sometimes they refer back to their original supporter, but more likely they refer back to the systematic process which had enabled them to achieve their first goal. They are empowered to risk swimming in deep water on their own in the search for a solution. Thereby their individual creativity is further stimulated.

It is debatable whether dyslexia enhances creativity. The very successful dyslexic composer Dr. Nigel Clarke (2008) has said that music was the only thing he could do and that he therefore was so focussed on it that he was not distracted by other possibilities. He added that most things can be achieved with hard work and technology. However, in his immersion in both of these of these areas, he seemed unaware that he actually has a very special innate talent which may originally have been totally uninfluenced by his focus, hard work or technology. Nevertheless, current brain research suggests there could be connections between dyslexia and creativity. Whatever is concluded, the scaffold of the learning process is still required for creativity in any area to be fostered and released.

References:

Gardner Howard (1987) Frames of Mind (2nd edition): The Theory of Multiple Intelligences. Fontana

Miles T & Westcombe John, Ditchfield Diana (2008) Music and Dyslexia: A Positive Approach. Wiley

Continental Drifting: Dyslexia rocks – literally

Jon Adams

Is been a few years since first writing for the B.D.A. handbook and my life has evolved in a myriad of directions, unseen at that point, coming almost full circle to combining the two 'creative loves' of my childhood, Geology and Art. I did get close in the 80's, when I embarked on my illustration career with companies like Shell and Hamlyns, and at times they have both come close to an 'extinction event', but my latest commission, 'Look About', is conceptually combining both of these and driven creatively by my supposed impairments.

At the age of six I knew I was to be an artist: I felt it, tasted it within me, but I also had to be the geologist I dreamed of being too. I felt instinctively 'drawn' to the natural systems I saw evidence of around me and the 'collecting/ collating' of them soon became solidified. It was on the frequent 'family trips' to the Lake District that I soon learnt that I could 'read the landscape' even before I could 'read about' the landscape. The untold tales of long lost lands, timescales and the animals they subversively contained, hidden and waiting for translation, started to obsess me. It was natural for me to see 'in 3D': all those layers beneath my feet and the secrets they contained came to life: corals and warm seas, cold snow-filled walks along the shores of Coniston water, or volcanic mayhem helter-skelter down the slopes at Borrowdale. I wanted to know more, I had to know more, but was never completely satisfied with the answers I was getting. I also realised at that point I had to learn to read, as my parents, friends and randomly asked visitors to the hotel soon grew bored of my continual questions. I had to learn to be self-dependent, reliant and enquiring: skills invaluable now. I had to learn to read.

It took a while, but it has started a 'internal paradox' at school that has remained with me ever since, which I was reminded of only last week when someone asked me 'How come I could spell long complex 'dinosaur' names in Latin, but not simple words like 'rabbit' or 'sense'. This blatant contradiction did cause trouble at school, mainly due to the misunderstandings of the education system at that time (1970's) when I was labelled and subsequently bullied as 'learning disabled'. I knew I could 'learn' but evidently 'writing' counted more and I soon had the word 'lazy' added to the above badges. I did however, draw constantly. When in trouble, this and my self-belief seem to have always saved me.

I never went to art college: my 'art career' abruptly terminated in my last year at junior school and from then on I kept it underground. I did, however, collect fossils and was drawn into that world completely. The drawing skills helped me to succeed at University, but my biggest gift was being able to see and work in 3D. I stumbled through my time quite 'unsociably', gaining my degree and taking a year out working at the Barbican Art Gallery before starting a Doctorate on sharks. Over that period I changed, and the desire to 'make' things came to the surface during one show and I started drawing again. Due to a mix of the bullying at school and my undiagnosed Aspergers, I was not a well person when it came to being with people. So how did I overcome this? Using lateral and other ways of thinking unique to a dyslexic – that applied creativity again- I time charted/ mapped my future directions out. *(A gift I still use every day)*

Forgoing the fish, I started working for a print company in their studio and progressed to freelance in a few years, illustrating for some large companies. I had a unique advantage, not only as an artist, but also as a scientist, having a grasp and an understanding of what I was asked to draw. After my dyslexia came to light in the late 90's, I changed tack, branching into writing and music, but as a 'person' I was still not ready. After a few years finding out who and what I was, I realised I could do anything I wanted. I did not have to hold back any ideas, but it was up to me to do it – just like at school. I acknowledged my broken past, the strengths, the weaknesses and so autobiography seemed 'fair game' to create work from, not to make sense of or to be overtly political, but to create solid bedrock to 'mine' and raise awareness on the way.

Determination and a self-imposed regime of learnt 'sociability' has led to many opportunities, as has following an instinct for creativity. I did my first geological artwork in 2006 – a copper map with stones which, after a 2 year gallery tour, sold. Next Pallant House Gallery where, when I was offered a solo show, I rashly said I would geologically reinterpret my life history. It worked and 16 cases of 'specimens' later, the show was a turning point for me in several ways in terms of increasing my confidence and obtaining further commissions. Somehow I found myself firmly entwined from the start in the Cultural Olympiad of which my latest project is a part.

*Briefly, **Look About** is a two-year R&D mapping and collecting project, gathering and making in digital & analogue media an intimate and 'Autobiostratigraphic' response to the London 2012 Cultural Olympiad. Mapping each day - looking at Inclusion, diversity and accessibility, all to be transformed and concealed within layers of geological metaphor, all woven within a major touring show, map and publication in 2012.*

So what is 'dyslexia' creativity? Is it only ability or skills in the arts (all branches, not just visual) or is it deeper? Is it a way of thinking, an invaluable 'core' skill that can be applied to a range of subjects? I tend towards the latter as both a 'heritable' and learnt skill of creative thinking that confers a responsibility on us not to squander it. This is only one part of the story, as being dyslexic does not automatically assure 100% artistic creativity, but it does raise the odds. We are the sum of all the parts that make us, including our experiences, good and bad, that have been influenced by being dyslexic.

For example, the United Kingdom, as we know it now, is made of distinctly different elements that have become 'welded' together due to the wandering and splitting apart of the continents over geological time. We can see something like this within ourselves - for example Dyslexia is just one 'region' of the 'supposed impairment 'supercontinent'; a 'dual tone' alongside my Aspergers and the learnt experiences that make me. I am only now able to express and try to systematise/ make sense of the layers of events that have brought me to this point in time.

Sometimes we just need learn to develop and apply this way of thinking subconsciously to any subject including the sciences. We have always valued unique and lateral thinkers who can 'see' the unseen and make leaps forward in critical thinking in all subjects. I think we can safely say that we 'see' the world differently, and to me this advantage far outweighs the deficiency in literary skills I may or may not be 'seen' to have.

To me drawing and thinking in 3D are 'primal' skills, writing and spelling are not.

Jon Adams, *Artist in Residence University of Portsmouth.*

Jon Adams is the project lead artist and geologist for Accentuate, the London 2012 Legacy Programme for the South East. Accentuate is funded by Legacy Trust UK, creating a lasting legacy from the London 2012 Olympic and Paralympic Games across the UK, SEEDA and the Regional Cultural Agencies.

Technology

Support Software for Dyslexics

Bernard Sufrin

Assistive Technology is specially designed computer hardware and software which helps people with special needs (including dyslexia) to be more efficient and independent at home, in education, and in the workplace. It often enables better use of mainstream technology.

In this article, adapted from materials on the B.D.A. New Technologies Committee website, we discuss support software for dyslexics. If you can, you should yourself spend some time browsing the site: **http://bdatech.org**.

Conventional Support for Writing

Word processing programs have made a major difference to many dyslexic users. They can help with writing in education, work and leisure activities. They can also be helpful for supporting the writing process (getting your ideas organised), and also for those who find presentation or handwriting a problem.

Word processing is a key written communication tool used in schools, colleges and many work situations. It enables easy drafting and editing. Users can move written text around the page easily, using facilities such as delete, cut, copy and paste.

There is no pressure to worry about rewriting texts many times over to get a neat piece of writing. Word processed text always looks pleasing. It is particularly helpful in schools and colleges when pupils and students can type longer pieces of work or essays. They are easier for their teachers to read, too.

It can be useful to use the same word processing software at home as is used in school or work. The best known such software is MS Word; it is sold with some computers, or can be easily purchased. The free-of-charge LibreOffice program (the successor to OpenOffice), can easily be downloaded, and is these days compatible with MS Word.

Some users like to word process, but type very slowly. Both Word and LibreOffice have text-prediction (sometimes called auto-completion) facilities built in, though these can take some getting used to. Depending on the version you use they may also have tools that will auto-correct or auto-complete words that are problematic for poor spellers. Some versions provide different coloured text/backgrounds, spelling and grammar support, text highlighting, and thesaurus facilities. All modern versions provide a means of annotating documents with short notes, and of recording changes made to documents; both facilities are useful for collaborative writing.

Talking Word Processors

Some word processors have a speech facility to enable users to hear the words and sentences as they are being typed. The program uses synthesised (robotic sounding) speech. This can help accuracy and reassure users that the content makes sense.

Many such programs offer a range of voices to choose from. They are used in many schools especially at KS 1, 2 & 3. Some programs will read toolbars and spellchecking menus, for example Write:OutLoud. Textease also combines the use of a talking word processor with other desktop publishing tools.

Some talking word processors have an on-screen word bank facility, which can save typing time. Word banks offer lists of regularly used words or subject vocabulary. Users click on the words they need from the list and it is entered into the text they are composing.

This saves typing time and problems with spelling. Users can listen to the words before selecting the one they need. They can also create their own personal lists to use in the word banks.

Some dyslexic students with strong visualisation skills benefit from using a talking 'rebus' word processor, where words are linked to symbolic representations. The symbols provide good support for preparing and editing work, but can be removed before the final printout. Rebuses are more effective spellcheckers and provide positive feedback for incorrect homonyms.

Voice or Speech Recognition Software.

Voice or speech recognition software enables users to speak the words they want to word process. This can be a useful option especially for older pupils, students and adults. However, it may not be as easy as it sounds; it takes time and training, and it is not very appropriate for use in the classroom. But it can be valuable for producing extended pieces of work in a quiet environment or at home.

Support for Reading

Text to Speech software is useful for dyslexic people, who:

- read slowly or with difficulty;
- have visual stress when reading;
- want feedback when writing;
- want help with spotting errors when proof-reading
- benefit from the multisensory experience of seeing and hearing.

Many modern mainstream computer operating systems, such as Apple's OS/X and Microsoft's Windows, provide text to speech tools free of charge. And since the advent of e-Books and relatively cheap e-Book readers with voice output, such as Amazon's Kindle, things are looking much better than they used to for dyslexics who need to have text read to them and don't want to spend a lot of money.

These tools, often displayed as an extra toolbar, enable any text selected on the screen to be spoken. Unlike the early robotic sounding voices, most of the latest tools deliver excellent human sounding speech, and many are available in regional accents. But some tools still have an infuriating tendency to mispronounce uncommon words.

Text to speech is said to be most helpful when individual words are highlighted on the screen as they are spoken. Dyslexic people say this focuses their attention and helps their understanding of the content.

Can I have a list of useful software?

People often ask for a list of suggested technologies and items of software to help with areas of dyslexic difficulty. This appears to be a simple question; but it is actually impossible to respond to it with a simple answer.

Why? Mainly because, as those with experience of using supportive software are only too well aware, it needs to be chosen and used to suit the needs of each individual person. Technology cannot provide a "one size fits all" solution since one person's dyslexic difficulties are rarely identical to another's.

Choosing technology to suit the needs of the individual.

Technology can be used with enormous benefits, but some users have been deterred by their previous unsuccessful experiences. They may have struggled with an earlier version of a piece of software or hardware that was not set up adequately. Sometimes this kind of problem can be overcome by appropriate training; but it can also occur because the technology chosen just did not suit the individual. It is only by observing how a person works that one can really obtain an understanding of the needs that must be met for him/her, hence gain an idea of how to begin to meet them.

Bernard Sufrin, *Fellow & Tutor in Computation*
Worcester College, Oxford

A 'Technology Toolkit' – one of your 'Tools of the Trade'

Mick Thomas

Tools of the Trade

All teachers will agree, in principle, that the school curriculum should include alternatives to make it accessible and applicable to students who have different learning styles, abilities, and disabilities. All classrooms will, as a matter of course, have a set of resources on hand for pupils to use when reading and writing. A Technology Toolkit should also be some of the 'tools of the trade' that are available for all students to use when they need, or want to.

The Technology Toolkit should include, at least, a choice of text-reading software, word-prediction software, concept mapping software and a variety of alternative input devices such as keyboards and mice.

Theset tools of the trade will provide useful support for all students, but may be vitally important for some students, as they may be the only way that they can produce work to the required standard.

Text-reading and Word-prediction software

From their earliest days in school, pupils will want to record their ideas and activities in words and pictures.

Teachers know that communicating ideas in writing, whether by hand or using a word processor, is a very complex task. The student needs not only to know what it is they are trying to express in words, but also they need to be able to spell all the words they need and to use the correct ones to fully explain and communicate their thoughts and ideas. A basic word processor can therefore offer a lot of support for early writers, for dyslexic pupils and for those who struggle to control a pencil.

Pupils who have a physical or motor impairment, and pupils who have dyslexia or other specific learning difficulty, may find handwriting difficult. As they get older and their work becomes more complex, they are likely to want more sophisticated software to support the production of projects, homework and presentations.

There are many opportunities for improving the quality and quantity of student writing through the use of technology. While some teachers may criticise software programs that provide spelling and grammar checkers that could lessen students' reliance on their own ability, research shows that students who have access to word processing programs to develop their writing skills are able to provide higher quality results than without.

Research also shows that speech-enhanced word-processors have made a significant contribution to supporting students with literacy difficulties. Having auditory feedback where the word processor 'speaks' each letter, word or sentence can enable improved access for many pupils, including those with visual and specific learning difficulties such as dyslexia.

For pupils with severe dyslexia or impaired cognitive development, an on-screen grid or word bank can also help them to communicate their ideas. On the other hand, they can also be very limiting for writers whose ideas far outstrip their ability to type words on a keyboard.

Simon is a Year 5 pupil struggling to develop his spelling skills despite considerable learning support. His reading is in advance of his spelling, so he is poorly motivated and frustrated because of his difficulties with writing. He recently had Claro Read installed on his laptop computer. This is a toolbar that is closely integrated with Microsoft Word and Internet Explorer, and enables practically any text to be spoken aloud. Claro Read has completely re-motivated him. Words are spoken back to him as he types them and this improves the accuracy of his work. He now produces greater length, better quality and high precision. His behaviour, which was a cause for concern, has improved and there is a noticeable increase in his self-esteem. He has also become less reliant on adult support because the talking word processor has enabled him to correct more of his own work himself as he goes along.

He was also introduced to a typing program at home. This involved daily ten-minute sessions using a typing package to improve his typing skills. He was encouraged to carry out his homework on his home computer, bringing to school his first and final drafts for comparison. He continues to have small-group teaching support, sometimes using spelling programs on the computer alongside more traditional methods.

Word prediction, as found in Claro Read, offers the students a list of suggested words as soon as they type in the first few letters. Assuming that their desired word is in the list, they can then select the whole word using a mouse or press of a function key, rather than having to complete it using the keyboard. This is useful for pupils who have difficulty in typing large amounts of text, or whose spelling is so poor that they rarely manage more than a handful of words on screen.

Word prediction software often comes with a range of dictionaries and word lists and also the opportunity to add your own lists, so it can be used to support any area of the curriculum or tailored very specifically to a student's own vocabulary.

Predictive software also 'learns' the user's vocabulary, so the more it's used, the better it adapts to the user.

Ben has been diagnosed as dyslexic. He appears to be a visual text learner whose reading ability is better than his spelling. He is able to initiate words but gets lost in the middle; however he can usually recognise the word he wants from a list. Most of his work is differentiated to enable him to record successfully by hand; sometimes he uses the word processor on the class computer in conjunction with Claro Read and Claro WordBank. He is able start words and then select from the on-screen wordlists and this helps him to improve the quality and quantity of his work - plus he now has an enhanced sense of achievement.

Visual concept-organization software

Creating a Concept Map enables pupils to focus their thoughts, organise ideas and include text notes, graphical and media content. Students can plan revision, reports, essays and presentation content in a more spontaneous but controlled manner. Concept-mapping software can be used by all students to organise and present information. Concept Maps allow a user to focus on bringing together thoughts and related content in various formats, and are a recognised way to maximise learning potential, improve problem solving, enhance research and aid revision for all students.

Ellie has difficulty with organising and presenting her ideas, so she uses 'Claro Ideas' to allow her to gather her ideas and convert them into an action list; this is a major advantage for her as her disability impairs her ability to plan efficiently. She also uses the software to plan projects such as essay writing, holiday preparation and to explain her science experiments.

Claro Read, Claro Ideas, Claro WordBanks are part of The Learning Access Suite 2012 which is available from MicrolinkPC (**www.microlinkpc.com**). The Learning Access Suite package offers schools and colleges a comprehensive set of reading, writing and study skills support tools. This unique collaboration between software provider Claro Software, and Microlink PC will soon be re-launched as Learning Access Suite 2012. The Learning Access Suite 2012 licence allows for unlimited use in an educational setting, and offers new and effective software tools for upper primary pupils, secondary school students, teachers, and home users, as well as students who are learning English as an additional language.

The Claro Learning Access Suite includes a wide range of facilities to make reading, writing and studying so much easier.

Mick Thomas
Head of Education
Microlink PC (UK) Ltd
Microlink House
Brickfield Lane
Chandlers Ford
Eastleigh
SO53 4DP

Mob: +44 (0)7501-469000
Web: **www.microlinkpc.com**

Integrated technology – Or how to make the most of "Text-to-Speech Plus"

Dr Ian Smythe

Once upon a time, text to speech software meant exactly what it said on the box – Software that took text from the computer and converted it to speech. But things have moved on since then, which was not so long ago.

Firstly, we have lost the box! Although statistics are not available, in a culture that is now used to downloading software, many individuals now prefer to download it directly, having paid for it online. This is mostly a good thing, except when you need to reinstall it on a new machine, and cannot find the software security code!

When it comes to the software, the traditional approach was to have a piece of software which would either read the file or the screen (possibly with intermediate optical character recognition – OCR), and convert that text into the spoken word. The voice could be a free voice (such as Microsoft) or a commercial voice. These functions help us immediately recognise two important, and separate, aspects of text to speech software - the "interface" and the "voice." This important distinction allows us to understand how it is possible to have many different voices with one "interface" and how it frees us from one fixed (and often limiting) solution.

The interface is the real controller. It may be considered the link between the written word and the sound output. It is the part which finds the right sound to match what is on the screen. But it is also so much more than that. And this is the part that we need to look at here.

All too often technology is specified as "You need this" when the needs have not been clearly identified. Therefore, let us start by asking what are the most common uses of Text To Speech (TTS).

- reading an electronic document such as word or pdf;
- reading text on the internet;
- proofreading your own work;
- checking pronunciation of a word or phrase;
- reading email and chat;
- hearing how some English words are pronounced correctly;

These may be books, web pages, documents, or any form of written word that can be made available electronically.

But now let us consider the associated functions

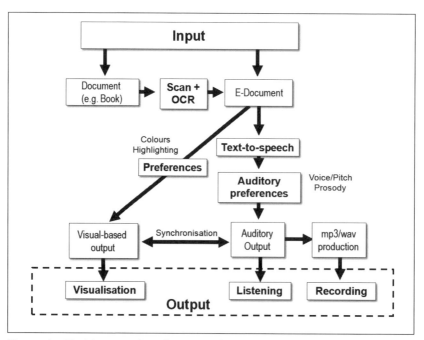

Figure 1 – Text to speech software package

If we look at Figure 1, we can begin to identify a number of different components that are now integrated as standard into many text-to-speech applications, whether they are the computer or USB based type. The latter may be particularly important if you move between computers, especially when some of the functions are missing. This can be particularly annoying if you are forced to use a "new" computer for an examination, and the system is not what you are used to.

The inclusion of all this software together has made it considerably easier for many students, now that they have a one stop shop. However, due to a lack of training (both of the students, and those providing the training!) many of the functions are often not explored. In the following sections we shall briefly highlight some of the functionality, and how it can be varied.

Scan + OCR

This is particularly useful when you have a document that cannot be accessed by the TTS software. The obvious examples are when you have a paper-based document, such as a book or journal. Some pdf documents are also saved in a manner that cannot be read. You may also have screen grabs (websites, ppts or other) which need converting to make them accessible to the reader, or the text itself is only provided as an image (e.g. a jpg).

Text-to-speech

This refers to the interface, whether it is a toolbar, cut and paste, browser-based or other type. It controls what can happen in terms of the auditory and visual experience. But it may also contain many other functions some of which may override the system or program settings. Of particular note are those that can have pop-up explanations, such as spellcheckers, dictionaries and translations as well as other functions such as word prediction and homophone checking.

Auditory preferences

There has always been some form of control over text-to-speech. But people rarely use this as they do not know that it exists, or they believe it is too difficult to access. Here are some of the aspects that you can "adjust", but you will have to look at your specific software to know if this is possible!

Changing the voice – It may seem obvious but few people realise that not only does the software often come with several voices, but you could add your own preference. For example, Cereproc (**www.cereproc.com**) offers English voices with accents that claim to be American, Irish, West midlands, Southern as well as Scottish.

Changing speed – The ability to adjust the speed that the software at which the words are spoken is one of the most useful functions. Some software does not make it easy to access this, but usually it is included somewhere, and may even have a simple shortcut. By knowing how to quickly adjust it, you can optimise it for a given document. You can also use it for different types of "reading" such as fast for "skimming" and slow when comprehension of all aspects is important.

Sound recording – Most of the commercial versions now offer the opportunity to save the text as a sound file. Some use the highly compressed mp3 format, while others use the much larger wav files. Some but not all of these TTS software have the option to create multiple files from one document. If the only option is to create a single sound file, it can be problematic to find a given paragraph. If however, the document is saved as a series of mp3 files, it is as easy to find the specific paragraph as it is to browse through songs on an mp3 player.

Change pronunciation – Sometimes a word may not be in the voice dictionary (modern voices store whole words and not just parts of words, hence the large file sizes) or it is pronounced wrongly. This is particularly true of names and places. If the word is heard regularly, it may be desirable to tell the software how to pronounce the word correctly the next time it is encountered. For this there is usually a special menu. Unfortunately it can sometimes take a lot of effort to find the right combination of letters so that the word is pronounced correctly.

Sound adjustment – This can be done inside the software, but it is often easier to do it from the computer volume control.

Visual preferences

Highlighting text as it is spoken – For many, using text highlighting is an obvious function and they always turn it on. However, if it highlights every word one by one, it can be very distracting, since the eye is drawn to each one, instead of concentrating on comprehension of the whole passage. If used to highlight the whole sentence or paragraph, this may be useful to track where you are within the text.

Typeface and font size – These are usually simple overrides to the document creation software such as Microsoft Word, and the same rules about choosing your preferred typeface and font size apply as when you are producing any document.

Leading and kerning – Spacing between lines and between letters can make a lot of difference to many dyslexic individuals. However it is easy to go too far! Increasing the gap between lines will make it easier to distinguish between lines, but too close together and it is difficult for the eye to easily follow to the next line. Varying the space between letters can make it easier to identify letters, but may make it more difficult to distinguish the gaps between words. These can only override in a document you are producing, such as Word. They cannot override pdfs or the browser.

Colour of the font and background–Some software, especially the cut and paste type (e.g. Balabolka) offers the option to change the colour of the background, as well as font colour. This is worth exploring, especially if you are not working in Word or similar where you can change background colours.

Conclusions

There is little doubt that there will continue to be a push for a "one-stop-shop" solution. But people have found that having everything in Google Docs was overwhelming. It is better to learn a little here and a little there, and bring it all together later. The same is true with the technology. No dyslexic individual is going to learn all the functionality in one training session. It is better to have a brief introduction, and slowly introduce additional functionality as and when the others are mastered.

Only in this way can we be sure that the full advantages of this software can be exploited.

Dr Smythe is a Visiting Professor in International Literacy at the School of Education, University of Wales Newport.

© Ian Smythe, *2011*

Free resources from update on EU projects

Dr Ian Smythe provides a brief review of dyslexia-related resources that have been made available recently through EU projects.

Introduction

In the UK we are (relatively) fortunate as there are many dyslexia-related resources available. But this is not true of countries and languages across Europe. Fortunately the EU sees this, and has funded a number of projects which provide valuable resources in different languages. And of course with the working language almost always being English, there are also English language resources produced within these projects. In the following pages we shall look as some of them in brief, and highlight what free resources may be available for parents, for teachers and for dyslexic individuals.

Adystrain (http://www.adystrain.project-platform.eu/)

ADysTrain is aimed at trainers in the field of adult training and for high-level personnel in leadership positions as well as high and mid-level management. Its purpose is to help employers become aware of dyslexia and how it may affect their workforce. The information will help employers to address the needs of dyslexic people by making them aware of the "reasonable adjustments" they may need to make, particularly in relation to workplace training, as well as indicating what benefits dyslexic people may bring to the workplace.

The principle project outcome was a series of e-books on dyslexia, how it may affect the workforce, and how to support the dyslexic individual (N.B. The web link provides an online version. The pdf versions are still available through **www.ibisconsultants.info**)

Caldys2 (**www.caldys2.eu**)

Learning foreign languages is very important to all, but it is more difficult for some of us. Traditional teaching methods are often less useful as their methods are discouraging for many dyslexic students. This project aims to engage the beginner, or re-engage the formerly alienated dyslexic language learner – no matter what age, or academic level - to learning.

Through its website, the project offers:

- Fun, dyslexia-friendly language learning games
- Editing tools to personalize content by teachers and parents
- Training for teachers and parents on dyslexia friendly language teaching with appropriate assistive technology

Although originally designed for learning English, the games can be adapted to learn any language, including English literacy skills for those with English as their first language.

Dessdys (**www.dessdys.eu**)

The Dessdys project is an international cooperation for supporting dyslexic individuals, by developing study skills support material for teachers, parents and professional helpers of students with dyslexia in 6 partner countries from all over Europe. The project built upon the experiences in other projects, to offer resources to help the dyslexic individual by means of specifically developed resources. These resources are:

- A study skills book, including sections on
- Using Assistive technology
- Reading and writing
- Listening and note taking
- Examinations
- Time management
- Templates for key activity

- A guide for tutors

Dys2 (**www.dys2.org**)

DYS 2.0 offers motivating and stimulating learning environment for a carefully selected range of skills known to be important for young dyslexic adults. The learning games address seven areas of particular importance for skills development:

- Auditory Discrimination
- Auditory Memory
- Auditory Sequence
- Visual Discrimination
- Visual Memory
- Visual Sequence
- Spatial Position

The principles behind the learning games are not specific to any given language – they will work for all individuals across Europe. The learning games have been developed in collaboration with young dyslexic adults as well as with those who train them. The main purpose of using the learning games is to support the development of vocational skills and life chances for young dyslexic adults and to provide a new kind of resource for trainers.

Dyscovering II (http://www.projectdyslexia.org/)

The aim of this project is to provide support to parents, teachers and dyslexic individuals themselves to ensure that the transition between schools is smooth and that they have the opportunity to reach their potential in the new learning environment.

This project designed a system to prepare a dyslexic child for transition from primary to secondary school. This will be achieved through a comparison of alternative practices in partner countries, and development of a model of best practice that may be widely used.

The core of the project was development of an Individual Support Plan (ISP) that not only provides details of the history of the child and of their needs, but also provides information for both the new secondary school and parents on how best to support the child during transition. It includes a checklist for identification of difficulties and an associated manual which will be the basis of development of the ISP and support for these individuals when they enter secondary school.

Dyslang (www.dyslang.eu)

The primary aim of this project is to develop and implement an e-learning course and best practice guide for teachers and parents to support the multilingual dyslexic individual in learning an additional curriculum language. The course will be made available free during the project, and for a small fee after the project, which will ensure its sustainability beyond the life of the funding. The project is led by the British Dyslexia Association.

The project will address the central concern of providing an inclusive learning environment which can be offered to those normally excluded from the curriculum. This will be achieved through appropriate support of the teachers and the resources produced to provide an opportunity to learn another language in school that is not the principle language of teaching, nor their first language.

The project will address the concerns listed above in the following ways:

1. It will help dyslexia pupils by empowering their teachers

2. It will provide the teachers with the training that they need

3. It will develop resources within the training to provide specialist knowledge

4. It will provide examples of best practice

5. It will raise awareness of the issues.

Dyslexia Veto (www.dyslexia-veto.org)

The project DYSLEXIA VETO - Dyslexia Friendly Quality Mark for Vocational, Education and Training Organisations – aims to test and adapt the Dyslexia Friendly Quality Mark criteria developed by the British Dyslexia Association (B.D.A.) for vocational organizations in the other countries of the project (Bulgaria, Italy, Hungary and Romania) with a view to improving its impact and performance in a vocational context.

Project specific aims:

- To facilitate and enable dyslexia friendly VET training/ education for young dyslexic individuals at possible risk of becoming disengaged from education.

- To improve the efficiency, effectiveness and responsiveness of the B.D.A. DFQM best practice in a multicultural society with a view to improving its impact and performance in a vocational context.

- To make the B.D.A. DFQM applicable for use across Europe to help equip dyslexia organisations to improve Dyslexia Friendly best practice in partner countries.

The project is led by the British Dyslexia Association.

Embed (www.embeddyslexia.eu)

EMBED - Embedding Dyslexia-Responsive Practices in Lifelong Learning - is an international project to support the dyslexic individual all over Europe by promoting better dyslexia provision in education, vocational training systems and in employment.

The specific outcomes made available through the Embed project Portal are:

1. Dyslexia Identification On-Line Test to help identify possible dyslexia related problems in their children or pupils.

2. Dyslexia Needs and Audit tool designed to assist in the identification of existing knowledge and awareness of dyslexia related issues.

3. Dyslexia Support Training Tool, e-Book designed to help identify key competencies for supporting dyslexic individuals.

4. Technology to support Dyslexic Individuals that has been developed throughout Europe mainly, but not exclusively, in the framework of previous and current EU's funded projects.

Isheds (**www.isheds.eu**)

The iSheds project provides resources and support for dyslexic students in Higher Education in Central Europe and the Balkan region, but also provides these same resources in English.

These resources include:

- Self-assessment tool for the dyslexic student
- E-learning for dyslexic students
- E-learning for those who support dyslexic students
- Free online Concept Mapping
- Free online Reminders system
- Policy reviews and checklists

Conclusion

The above projects provide many of the resources that parents and teachers need, at least in some of the key areas of support. It is far from a complete list, and many others may be found, and more are being funded every year.

If you need more details about any of these, please contact those highlighted on the web sites, or Dr Ian Smythe – **ianssmythe@gmail.com**.

Dr Smythe is a Visiting Professor in International Literacy in the School of Education, University of Wales, Newport. He has also been involved with more than ten dyslexia-related EU funded projects.

Further Education and Higher Education

Support for dyslexia in college and in university

Elizabeth Symes

For any student, making the move into Further Education (FE) or Higher Education (HE) is an achievement in itself. But it is all the more so for a student with dyslexia who has had to strive to achieve what tends to come more easily to others. However there has probably never been a better time to be a dyslexic student in FE/HE, since so much has been achieved in terms of identification and support for those who experience barriers to learning, in particular dyslexia. The purpose of this chapter is to outline some of the support available and to show how a proactive approach on your part can help you make the most of what is on offer.

Firstly it is important to recognise that students with dyslexia in FE/HE fall into two distinct categories. The first comprises those students who have been formally 'diagnosed' with dyslexia and who already have a Statement of Special Educational Need. The second is made up of students who have experienced difficulties with varying degrees of severity with their learning in school, but not recognised as dyslexic. They themselves, their families and even their teachers may have suspected that dyslexia was the cause but for one reason or another, their difficulties have never been fully identified. It is likely that in FE/HE settings the difficulties experienced by this second group will become more apparent. This is because the nature of study in FE and in particular HE settings is rather different from that of school, requiring a greater degree of self discipline, independent study and personal organisation as well as a much greater volume of independent reading.

The good news is that since 2001 the Special Educational Needs and Disability Act, SENDA, has required schools, universities and colleges to provide appropriate support for disabled students, including those with dyslexia. This means that not only do tutors *want* to help and support students with learning difficulties but also they are *obligated* to do so. SENDA places the following three obligations on educational institutions:

- Not to unreasonably discriminate against disabled students
- To ensure that reasonable adjustments are made in order to make learning accessible. Note that you will still be required to meet the same *academic standards* as other students.
- To be anticipatory, requiring planning ahead to be prepared for the needs of future students.

These days, all colleges and universities have a 'Learning Support Department', details of which can be found on their websites.

Students who think that they may have a difficulty that has not previously been diagnosed will find it much easier to obtain a full assessment of their needs once they are at college or university. They should approach their Learning Support Department as early on in their course as possible; they may also be encouraged to do so by their tutors.

Getting information before making an application

The more you can find out before making an application to a college or university, the better. One way is to visit the website and to get hold of a prospectus in advance; but even better is to attend an Open Day. A thoughtful and caring institution will ensure that the Learning Support Department is represented at the Open Day events so that you can find out firsthand about the support available to you. You could also email or telephone the leader of the course or programme in which you are interested, to make specific queries.

Making an application

When you make an application on your UCAS or other application form you will have the opportunity to disclose your disability. Often at this point a college/university will pass on your details to its Learning Support Department who will send you an information pack. Disclosure should not put you at any disadvantage; the criteria on which your application will be judged will be exactly the same as for any student who has not disclosed a disability. A good reason for disclosure is so that the college/university can then ensure that it is able to make the necessary reasonable adjustments to its interview processes to ensure that they do not discriminate against you.

Once you have accepted a place

If you are in receipt of a Statement of Special Educational Need, as soon as you accept the offer of a place you should contact the Learning Support Department at your chosen college or university to discuss your needs. Dyslexia and other Specific Learning Difficulties are considered to be disabilities in the context of Higher Education, and so you should be eligible to apply for the Disabled Students' Allowances (DSA). DSAs are funds that are used to pay for any additional study related support that you may need. This might include a note taker or study support tutor and could also include IT support, for example the provision of relevant specialist software for your computer.

The Learning Support department will help you with your DSA application, for which you will need an Educational Psychologist's report carried out after the age of 16. If your EP report is older than this the Learning Support department will arrange any necessary additional assessment to update your report so that you can make an application.

Support once you begin your studies

As part of the assessment process the Learning Support department will issue you with a Personal Learning Plan (PLP) which will give your tutors and the staff in your college/university library an outline of the reasonable adjustments that they can make to help you. Typically your PLP will request that you are able to record lectures, have lecture notes and handouts made available to you in advance, and have extended loan arrangements for books and other resources. Your PLP will also make recommendations about assessment and examinations.

Taking responsibility for yourself

The most successful students are proactive and take full advantage of all the support available. Here are some suggestions for ways in which you can do this:

- Discuss the content of your PLP with your course tutors and personal tutor if you have one;
- Let tutors know when you are going to record their lectures;
- Visit your library counter. It is likely that your PLP grants you additional library loan facilities but you will need to discuss these with the library staff who will issue them to you;
- Get to know your librarians and *don't* be afraid to ask for help. They can assist you to use the library and its facilities more easily and will help you to search for relevant journals etc when you need them for assignment work;
- Make sure you become familiar with your college/university virtual learning environment (VLE) which will provide a wealth of information and support. Often resources etc are put up in advance of lectures and these will help you to prepare in advance.
- Cooperate fully with your Learning Support tutor and those who are trying to support you;
- Make good use of the resources provided by your DSA. If you feel that you do not have the skills or knowledge to get the best from what you have got, then ask your Learning Support tutor for advice;
- Think about assessment and examinations in advance. If your course is assessed mainly by end of unit assignments, make sure that your sessions with your learning support tutor take into account your assessment calendar. If you need to negotiate coursework deadlines with your tutors, do so in advance. If you need to have special arrangements during

examinations, make sure that you discuss these in advance with the Examination's Officer;

■ Consider becoming a student representative for your course or programme so that you can have a voice to influence policy and practice – you can help to raise the issue of dyslexia by highlighting good practice within your institution and making suggestions for improvements.

Work based placements

Many courses involve work based placements, for example in hairdressing, teaching or social work. These course elements can be very rewarding and enjoyable because they provide you with the opportunity to put theory into practice. However, they can also be particularly daunting, if you find yourself in a situation where you feel that your particular difficulties and weakness are 'exposed' in any way.

Of course you are not under *any* obligation to disclose your dyslexia to the staff that you are working with on placements, but if you do not do so they are under no obligation to make any special arrangements for you. It is likely that there will be a student mentor involved in your supervision during placement as well as a college/university tutor who may visit from time to time. They can be very helpful in explaining to those in your work place how to address your needs. It is helpful to your mentor to know about the things that you find difficult so that they can support you more effectively. If they are made aware of your difficulties they will more readily notice and give you credit for the strategies that *you* put in place to help *yourself* and you will be seen as being proactive about your dyslexia. A word of warning however: Do not assume that they will necessarily be aware of your PLP! You may need to draw it to their attention.

If you have worries or concerns about issues related to your work based placement, then it is a good idea to discuss these with your course tutor and/or your Learning Support tutors in advance.

In conclusion

Colleges and universities have come a long way in the last 15 years in the ways in which they offer support to dyslexic students. However, it really is up to you to take full advantage of the support on offer. So go for it…and enjoy your studies.

The Quality Mark Experience

Alan Waugh

The Learner Support team at City College investigated pursuing the British Dyslexia Association Dyslexia Friendly Quality Mark over four years ago. An evaluation of our provision showed that there was a lot of good practice either being developed, or in some instances established. At that time we were in accommodation that spread over three sites and in buildings that were becoming old. The Coventry City Council had expressed that they wanted to pursue a 'Learning Quarter' in the City Centre, close to Coventry University, to include a Further Education establishment and a new secondary school and this was an opportunity to bring together the staff team in one modern provision.

This development has now seen City College provision sited at Swanswell with two new buildings, one specifically to meet the needs of our vocational provision in construction and engineering. City College also has a large Work Based Learning provision and provides national apprenticeship training in vehicle engineering and vehicle body repair to the Public Service Vehicle sector for clients such as Arriva and First bus companies.

Having just settled in to the new building, I read an article by Dr. Kate Saunders in the Contact magazine about the VETO project, inviting interested Further Education establishments to take part in the project. I discussed this with the team and we felt that this was the right time to pursue the Quality Mark, in our new surroundings, to be able to validate the good work that is being carried out by ourselves and our colleagues, highlighting the inclusiveness of Coventry's new college.

A particularly interesting feature for us was that this was to be a whole organisation approach, to include not just the academic staff, but also ensuring our business support colleagues were aware of the needs of our dyslexic learners and dyslexic colleagues and were able to use strategies to engage positively with dyslexia friendly practices.

Initial Evaluation

We were fortunate to have the support of our Vice Principal for Communications, People and Development who was involved in the first meeting with Kate. The first action plan showed that in Section 1 we needed to carry out an impact assessment on our policies to be dyslexia friendly. This has resulted in suitable amendments being made for ratification by the Board of Governors. The structure of our Learner Support team is such that we work closely with the Faculties and their management, and support for learners has always been recognised as essential, being a regular agenda item at management meetings and contributing to our key performance indicators.

City College has been a centre for delivery of the OCR qualifications for Teachers of Learners with Specific Learning Difficulties since 1998. We are fortunate to have on the team four Level 7 specialists carrying out assessments for exam arrangements, full diagnostic assessments for apprentice learners giving strategies for teaching and for the workplace, as well as assessments for Disabled Students' Allowance for those of our learners progressing to Higher Education.

This initial evaluation made us aware that we needed to be more proactive in our transition work. The sharing of information regarding our learners coming from school is valuable in setting strategies at the earliest opportunity. This is an area where we have made much improvement. We have also ensured that, where possible, we will support the learners in transition from college to their chosen progression route.

We were also aware that we needed to work with our teaching colleagues, giving them more awareness of suitable strategies for teaching and looking at resources we could use to help support understanding and achievement. For work based learners, we recognised that they needed to be able to have greater opportunities for showing their knowledge and skills through diverse methods of assessment. There was also the opportunity to provide advice and guidance to employers on how they can support their apprentices in the workplace with suitable adjustments.

The initial evaluation also highlighted that we need to be maintaining regular contact with outside agencies supporting learners and also with the parents and carers of our learners. It is an opportunity to extend the network of support and understanding needed in helping our learners to succeed.

Whole College Experience

The Quality Mark experience has made us realise that where much of the focus in supporting dyslexic learners is on the academic standards, there are other colleagues in the business support sections who need to be aware of the needs of our learners as they come in regular contact with them.

We have worked with the Personnel Department on ensuring that disclosure is encouraged for future employees at the application stage and that support needs will be met in the interview process. Dyslexia awareness is now included as part of the new staff induction and information is signposted on the Staff Intranet.

There are members of staff who have recently come forward asking for an assessment as they are involved in professional development courses within the college and have become aware that they may be experiencing a specific learning difficulty. This is dealt with confidentially and assessments are carried out by the specialist assessors within the Learner Support team.

Staff training days mean that colleagues are given training sessions by the college specialists. Regular training slots are now available in the college Professional Development Centre for all staff to access.

Positive aspects of the B.D.A. / VETO Quality Mark experience

I attended a meeting at the British Dyslexia Association offices in Bracknell in December 2009 and had the pleasure of meeting the European partners of the VETO project and Dr. Ian Smythe. I was obviously aware of the work of Dr. Smythe and looked forward to having access to the Learner Profiler that he has developed.

I have been working with dyslexic learners for over twelve years and have seen great leaps forward in our assessment and the recognition of dyslexia in this country. In conversation with the partners, it was fascinating to discuss the differences and to realise how far ahead we are.

The Learner Profiler was well received by our learners – and colleagues. We particularly liked the feedback and advice given to the learner and one teacher commented that it was useful for informing her of strategies to include in her teaching of her learners. It was user friendly and the instructions were clear.

The British Dyslexia Association produced a DVD for dissemination on the work of the VETO project and included material from City College. I included in this an extract from an apprentice carpenter whose portfolio evidence is filmed so he is able to tell his assessor how he has completed tasks. The employer is also there to corroborate his competence. We have made cameras that can be used for this purpose available to work based assessors.

The transition process is now robust and Learner Support Coordinators visit schools to meet with the school SENCO to share information. Itis hoped to expand this to include our support staff visiting schools to meet prospective college learners and to give them the opportunity to visit us, in order that informed choices can be made and that young people with dyslexia can be confident that support will be there for them.

I believe that this has been a good experience for the college and this will be shown in the improved experience for our learners. It has allowed us to look at our processes and to think about the evidence required to demonstrate that we have established good practice. We have been fortunate to have the support of dedicated colleagues and of our senior management and in that spirit I would hope that we will further develop and improve the learning experience for our dyslexic learners in our new home at Swanswell Centre, Coventry.

Alan Waugh, *Programme Area Manager Learner Support*

Study Skills for Dyslexic Students

Ros Lehany

For several years now there has been a debate about the terminology used to describe the specialist support given to dyslexic students in Higher Education. In January 2011 it was agreed to replace the term 'study skills' with 'specialist 1:1 support' in all guidance documents for the Disabled Students Allowance (DSA). This change was the culmination of several years' campaigning by professional groups working in the HE sector. The need to remove the term 'study skills' was first recognised when it became clear that there was a wide misunderstanding of what happens when a dyslexic student receives 1:1 support in Higher Education. It had become clear that many people believed such support sessions were run along the lines of a traditional study skills session.

Traditional study skills sessions are topic-centred and are offered at a wide level (sixth form, FE, HE and adult learning) to students of all abilities. A typical study skills session will take a topic such as 'Reading for Research'. The tutor will then talk through various strategies and approaches, handouts will be given to students and exercises will be completed, either in the session or later in the student's own time. Study skills can be delivered to groups or on a 1:1 basis. In practice, the support sessions that dyslexic students attend in HE are fundamentally different to this both in content and delivery.

In 2008 the Association of Dyslexia Specialists in Higher Education (ADSHE) produced their *Guidelines for Quality Assurance in Specialist Support for Students with SpLDs in Higher Education* (available at **www.adshe.org.uk**). A key element of the guidelines is the visual chart which goes some way to illustrate the complexity of the content of support sessions at this level. Ten main areas of support are identified, including traditional aspects such as academic writing, exam preparation, time management, but also areas such as addressing learner anxiety and establishing learning priorities. For each of these areas of support, a number of tasks that the student may have to complete are listed. For example, in academic writing the tasks include understanding what a question is asking, using academic language, understanding plagiarism, writing to a word count, outline and detailed planning, producing drafts and referencing. For each of these tasks there are a variety of strategies that might be appropriate for the student and again, under academic writing, these include the use of mind maps, understanding learning styles, verbalising, managing the behaviour cycle and engaging critical thinking skills. Finally, at every stage of support the tutor needs to be actively aware of the seven underlying principles of support. These seven principles are:

- meta-cognition
- multisensory approaches
- relevance
- motivation
- over learning
- 'little and often'
- modelling

If you consider this support as a 3D structure (rather like a chemical molecule), the student is at the centre surrounded by the topics. Each topic has branches representing the tasks that comprise this topic and for each of these tasks there is another set of links for the strategies that could be used. How each strategy is used must take account of the seven underlying principles. The content of support at this level is complex and to try to deliver it following the traditional study skills model described above is clearly going to be a daunting, if not impossible, task.

Support for students in HE is usually funded through the DSA which, following recommendations made in the student's needs assessment, specifies the number of hours of 1:1 support (additional hours can be applied for) and official guidance states that 'Individual 1:1 support… should…aim to develop the student's skills for autonomy in the learning environment' (BIS 2011 **www.practitioners.studentfinanceengland.co.uk** select Practitioner Resources, then Guidance Chapters). Therefore, an important change at this level of support is the amount of responsibility that now falls on the student. The support systems they may have had in place previously (e.g. school, parents) are not there and it is the student's responsibility to access the support that is available. The time management and organisational skills required to do this can in themselves be a challenge to many dyslexic students. For a considerable number of students university is the first time their dyslexic profile is identified and whilst for most this is a positive experience, students can still find coming to terms with their new 'label ' and identifying their support needs an additional element in an already stressful situation. Dyslexia coordinators and disability staff in universities work hard to encourage students to attend their first support session where many fears can be allayed and the nature of support at this level can be explained.

In the first session the student's responsibilities are clarified and the student is often asked to sign a learning agreement which sets out the responsibilities of the student and the tutor and covers issues such as cancellation protocols. The tutor and student will then work together to identify the learning priorities, always mindful that these are likely to change as the course progresses. Dyslexia support in HE is student-centred and work-load driven; students and tutors work on what is most important at the time and for the vast majority of dyslexic students the initial focus of support will be organisation and time management.

In the short term, students need to consider their weekly timetable; how they will prepare for lectures and organise their independent study. In the medium term, they will need to identify the first assessment point, identify the tasks they need to complete for this and when they need to achieve them by. An early support session often focuses on addressing these issues and the student will be expected to bring the relevant information with them and then, under the guidance of the tutor, draw up their own schedule and identify what they will do before the next session.

Subsequent sessions often follow the following structure:

- **Review** – did the student manage to meet the expectations of the last session? Identify what worked and what didn't work.
- **Respond to the student's needs** – what needs to happen now?
- **Focus on process** – how are they going to complete the task in hand?
- **Model & 'mentor' strategies using principles** – tutor introduces strategies and encourages the student to 'discover' effective practices
- **Discuss expectations** – identify what the student needs to do before the next session

HE support often involves using the student's current piece of work and it is very important that professional boundaries are observed; it is the first rule of dyslexia support that the tutor does not do the student's work for them. A tutor's role is to guide, direct and facilitate the embedding of skills in the task the student is working on. Students are under a great deal of pressure and have little motivation or time to work on tasks that have no direct relevance to them; if they cannot work on the task in hand they will not come for support. ADSHE guidelines state that 'students are responsible for developing their own learning processes and dyslexia tutors are facilitators' (ADSHE 2008: p11). The encouraging of independent learning is the most important task the specialist tutor has when supporting dyslexic students at any level but particularly in an HE context.

In order to develop independent learning, the student's individual cognitive profile and learning preferences must be prioritised and tutors have to be aware that what works for one student will not necessarily work for another. Each student is different and tutors have to use all their specialist expertise to identify appropriate strategies and techniques. There is little time for trial and error at HE level. Finally, changing the name from 'study skills' to 'specialist 1:1 support' does not mean that skills for studying are not being taught. Rather, the emphasis is that support is tailored to the student's individual profile and needs and further, that it is facilitated by someone who has the specialist training to understand how that particular student could become an independent learner.

Association of Dyslexia Specialists in Higher Education

The Association of Dyslexia Specialists in Higher Education (ADSHE) was set up to share knowledge and inform good practice in working with students with dyslexia, dyspraxia and other SpLDs in Higher Education. ADSHE has since expanded its influence significantly and now has an active role in addressing relevant issues at a national level.

ADSHE aims to:

- *Work towards establishing parity of provision so these students will be assured of appropriate support throughout the HE sector*
- *Establish commonly accepted codes of good practice*
- *Allow members to share experiences and overcome feelings of isolation*
- *Provide CPD for members*

Ten regional groups offer ADSHE members opportunities for CPD and networking.

Look out for details of our Annual Conference in June 2012 and other training events

If you are working with students in Higher Education please get in touch with us – through our website **www.adshe.org.uk**

or by emailing **adshedyslexia@yahoo.co.uk**

New Developments

Recent Developments

Mel Byrne

Collaborative work and changing times

Our children in schools today deserve the opportunity to fulfill their potential and learn the skills they need to succeed in later life. For many of our children with special educational needs this is not a given. For those of us in the SEN sector, we have made it our mission to ensure that this happens for all children. Is it really that complex an issue to make this happen?

The period following the White Paper : The Importance of Teaching, (DfE 2010) and the Green Paper, Support and aspiration: A new approach to special educational needs and disability, (DfE 2011), has given rise to much activity within the voluntary and community sector to ensure that the needs of our children and young people are met. There has been a stream of consultations and call for views by Government working parties. Various new initiatives are under way, including 'Achievement for All' and the Pathfinder pilots to provide support and guidance to schools under the remit of the new single Education Health and Care Plan.

There is an existing bank of expertise in special educational needs across the third sector and excellent teachers in schools who can make a real difference to all children and their education; the real tricky bit is how we marry these and provide the specialist support to those that need it at the right stage. Collaboration is the way forward but how do we ensure our children, young people, adults and families know what services are available?

Not only do those children and young people with special educational needs need support, but also the educational workforce engaging with our children; they need guidance too. We have recently seen the development of some excellent training materials, ranging from a whole school approach at very basic level aimed at the full complement of the school workforce, to Master's level aimed at the specialist teacher assessors. NASEN and The Specialist Schools and Academies Trust (SSAT) have collaborated on 'A whole school approach to improving access, participation and achievement', which provides training and resources via SENCOs to all schools. SENJIT, as part of The Institute of Education, have produced a set of on-line specialist resources commissioned by the Training and Development Agency (TDA) and the Inclusion Development Programme (IDP), and these materials remain a valuable resource for schools. These materials are freely available to all schools and have been produced collaboratively by specialist organisations within the voluntary and community sector.

The Dyslexia-SpLD Trust, The Autism Education Trust and The Communication Trust have each developed frameworks by which practitioners and school senior management teams can clearly gauge the knowledge and skills required to effectively and inclusively support the needs of our children and young people with SEN.

With approximately two million of all children in England having been identified with SEN, teachers need support on how to manage this.

There is much emphasis on synthetic phonics being the main approach to literacy teaching. With the impending phonics check for our children in Year One currently being piloted and due for implementation in 2012, it is clear that the Department for Education gives weight to this approach. It is agreed within the sector that decoding, while central, is not the only skill involved in reading and should not become the exclusive focus of teaching. With high quality synthetic phonics teaching, many children 'at risk' of literacy failures will respond well, but they may have problems later with more complex aspects of decoding, with reading fluently and with spelling.

So what about those children who do not make progress with good quality first teaching, high quality synthetic phonics teaching and the subtle changes put in place to accommodate those children with SpLD? They will need additional support outside of the classroom setting.

There are some very good intervention programmes outlined in Professor Greg Brooks' 'What Works for pupils with literacy difficulties?' (2007). If used correctly, these can boost progress and help most children to get back on track. Sir Jim Rose outlined the importance of personalizing learning by matching provision to meet individual needs (Rose 2009). This is reliant on using effective interventions that accelerate progress. For many of our children with specific learning difficulties such as dyslexia, a combination of approaches is key. There is not one particular method or resource that will meet every child's needs. 'Interventions for Literacy', an on-line resource produced by The Dyslexia-SpLD Trust, provides a useful navigation system for schools and parents to reference. There will, however, be a percentage of our children whose difficulties need addressing out of the classroom setting by a teacher with a specialist qualification.

We are in changing times following The Green Paper (DfE 2011) and we see new initiatives and pilots as a result of its content and aspirations. Primary Care Trusts and Local Authorities have been encouraged to come together to pilot the new single plan, the Education Health and Care Plan (ECHP), under the Pathfinder scheme. The voluntary and community sector plays a key role in advising and ensuring that the needs of our children are met under this process. They also play a key role in ensuring that our children with high-incidence, low severity SEN, are not missed under the revision of the Code of Practice.

Since the Rose Report (2009) we have had an injection of specialist teachers trained to provide expertise across the country. These specialist teachers are ready to support schools in the management of children and young people with specific learning difficulties and to provide direct support to those children with the greatest need. The key factor is that the teacher is suitably qualified and experienced at delivering a prescribed, multisensory, structured programme, using regular checks to monitor progress.

Throughout The Green Paper (DfE 2011) there is a message about giving parents and carers more choice and involvement in making decisions about their child's provision. This was reported clearly by Brian Lamb in his inquiry, 'Special Educational Needs and Parental Confidence' (2008) and by Rose (2009) in his report. If parents have the knowledge to support their children at home and throughout their child's education, their involvement and support can be significant to the child's progress and aspirations.

The Dyslexia-SpLD Trust is working on a collaborative project combining the knowledge and expertise of experts in the field to provide this valuable service to parents in the community. The two year project brings together The British Dyslexia Association, Dyslexia Action, Helen Arkell Dyslexia Centre and Springboard for Children, providing surgeries, workshops and parent forums across the country.

So, with quality first teaching, excellent continuing professional development for teachers in SEN, early intervention across all three waves of teaching, good information and guidance to parents and specialist teachers accessible to the school workforce, we should be able to achieve our aspiration of every child fulfilling their potential. After all, "education is the most powerful and successful cognitive enhancer of all" (The Royal Society 2011).

References:

Brooks G (2007) *What works for pupils with literacy difficulties? The effectiveness of intervention schemes* The Department for Children, Schools and Families

The Department for Education(2010) *The Importance of Teaching: The Schools White Paper 2010* The Stationary Office

The Department for Education(2011) *Support and aspiration: A new approach to special educational needs and disability* The Stationary Office

The Dyslexia-SpLD Trust(2010) *Interventions for Literacy* **http:// www.interventionsforliteracy.org.uk/ The department for Children, Schools and Families**

Lamb B (2008) *Lamb Inquiry: Special Educational Needs and Parental Confidence* The Department for Children, Schools and families

The National Strategies(2010) *Inclusion Development Programme (IDP)* **http://nationalstrategies.standards.dcsf. gov.uk/node/116691**

The National Strategies(2007) *Leading improvement using the primary framework: Quality first teaching* 00484-2007DOM-EN

http://nationalstrategies.standards.dcsf.gov.uk/node/64932

Rose J (2009) *Identifying and Teaching Children and Young People with Dyslexia and Literacy Difficulties* The Department for Children, Schools and Families

The Royal Society(2011) *Brain Waves Module 2: Neuroscience: implications for education and lifelong learning Science* Policy Centre

Dyslexia/SpLD Professional Development Framework

Lynn Greenwold

Background

Over the past decade there has been a steady increase in the number of professionals within a range of educational settings who have sought to increase and develop their knowledge and expertise in the teaching and support of pupils with dyslexia/SpLD. At the same time, the development of more inclusive settings and inclusive teaching has meant that all professionals are required to be able to deliver a curriculum that provides an effective education for all learners. In order to support this development, there has been a corresponding proliferation of different methods and routes through which the required knowledge and skills can be acquired. These include qualifications at undergraduate and post graduate levels, short courses and various other continuing professional development (CPD) opportunities. One consequence of this expansion has been that it can be somewhat confusing to professionals, as to the level of knowledge and skills needed for specific roles and what might be the best way to acquire the required level of competence. In order to help clarify this current situation and contribute to the implementation of some of the recommendations from the Rose Review, the Dyslexia SpLD Trust was commissioned to write a Framework for Best Practices.

The writing of the Framework began in November 2009. From the very start of the project, one of the aims was to ensure that a wide variety of stakeholders working in different settings and with a wealth of knowledge and expertise in the area of dyslexia/SpLD were invited to take part and contribute to the process of developing the structure and content of the framework. The stakeholders included representatives from the Department of Education, National Strategies, the Training and Development

Agency for schools, Local Authorities (LAs), universities, non-governmental organisations and training providers. A conference was held in March 2010 where participants were invited to contribute and share ideas, and this was followed up with a series of meetings with a smaller focus group to shape the final Framework.

Whilst considering the dyslexia/SpLD content of the Framework, it was recognised by those involved in the planning process, that for the Framework to be more effective it had to be compatible with and support, other related frameworks and the wider inclusion policy context. Consequently, various other frameworks also inform the content of the Best Practice framework, such as the Qualifications and Credit Framework; the Professional Standards for Teachers; the Speech, Language and Communication Framework; the Inclusion Development Programme and the Autism Education Trust framework, currently under development, among others.

Aims

For the first time within the field, the Framework encompasses the levels of knowledge and skills required to fulfil various roles across the workforce to support learners with dyslexia/SpLD. The Framework serves as a reference point in the creation and implementation of coherent and appropriate training, professional development and strategic planning across the education workforce. In doing so it will bring the following benefits to professionals, learners with dyslexia/SpLD and their families:

- Provide a simple and straightforward route map defining the knowledge and skills required at various levels and career points.
- Allow individuals within the education profession to identify and evaluate their training needs and those professionals with wider CPD responsibilities such as members of school leadership teams, governors, and LAs to identify, deliver and evaluate CPD.

- Provide guidance for the mapping and development of a range of qualifications to support learners with dyslexia/SpLD.

- Encourage clear academic and professional progression routes from initial qualification to post graduate level, for the workforce involved in supporting learners with dyslexia.

- Provide a common focus for organisations who are commissioning training programmes so that they appropriately address the specifically identified knowledge, understanding and skills as indicated through the framework.

Dyslexia-SpLD Trust Professional Development Framework

About

The Dyslexia/SpLD Professional Development Framework is an easy to use online tool that encompasses the levels of knowledge and skills required across the education workforce to support all learners with dyslexia/SpLD.

(+) About the Framework

(+) What are the benefits of using the Framework?

(+) How was the Framework developed?

(+) Start a self assessment

Figure 1:

Content

The Framework is available to be completed on line via the Dyslexia/SpLD Trust website. The knowledge and skills within the Framework is presented around six main strands as identified in Figure 1.

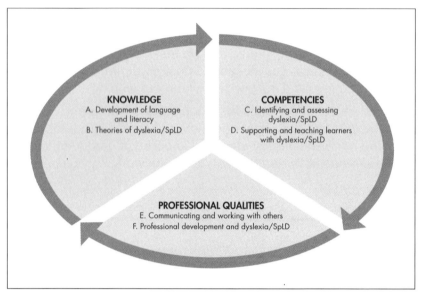

Figure 2: Dyslexia/SpLD Framework for Best Practices – Strands

For each strand individual competencies are allocated to one of five progressive stages of knowledge and levels of skill which correspond to specific roles across the workforce such as a teaching assistant, a Special Educational Needs Coordinator/Inclusion Manager or those professionals working in specialist and advisory roles working across many educational settings.

When first completing the Framework, an individual is requested to select the stage which is most appropriate to their role and from there they are presented with a number of statements from which they assess their individual level of knowledge and/or skill against the competency using a grading system. After completing the Framework, the individual is presented with a report that identifies strengths and those areas that might be a focus for further training and development. There will also be a link to suggestions for resources that could support the development of a particular skill or area of knowledge.

Timeline

The Framework is now being implemented as part of the Autumn Roll-out implementation phase. This includes incorporation in

the NASEN-Schools Network SENCo training package and the Achievement for All implementation programme, both being rolled out to all schools nationwide. After a successful review from a number of different professionals on a range of aspects including accessibility, relevance and effectiveness, a variety of stakeholder organisations have agreed to be part of a series of case studies. This includes local authorities, universities, training providers and schools. The case-studies will provide examples of how the Framework might be used to inform specific roles, targets for school improvement and appraisal processes. For providers of CPD, training and qualifications feedback is being sought on how the Framework offers a reference for informing the content and levels of training they deliver. Case-studies will also provide feedback to underpin the robustness of the framework, including adding to key documents, banks of teaching resources and workplace activities to embed effective CPD. Currently, provision of recommendations for appropriate courses is still under development. Please check the Dyslexia/ SpLD Trust website for further developments and feel free to explore the Framework for yourself in your own unique setting.

Finally, the members of the steering group would like to thank all the stakeholders and members of the focus group who have contributed so valuably to the process of writing the framework to date.

http://www.thedyslexia-SpLDtrust.org.uk/resources-professionaldevelopmentframework/

International

Dyslexia in FE/HE – International Comparisons

Dr. Gavin Reid

International comparisons, although useful, are always quite tricky. Are we really comparing like with like? Are the policies and practices associated with a given country really representative of that country? Even within countries such as the UK one will find disparities between different areas, even though all geographical areas are governed by the same national legislation. Having approached a number of colleagues on this subject from many countries however, it does seem that most are dealing with the same issues, although the approaches may differ. This is perhaps why international conferences, such as the World Dyslexia Forum in Paris in 2010, the B.D.A. International Conference, 2011 and the IDA annual conferences, are always popular and attract delegates from all around the globe.

Though policies and practice may differ (and they do!) the type of question parents and young people with dyslexia ask are usually similar. I have collected views from people with dyslexia in New Zealand, Australia, UK, Republic of Ireland, Kuwait, Cairo, Canada and the USA; and the similarities among the respondents is striking. There is still the shared view that if at all possible one should hide one's dyslexia. The medical model still predominates. This is supported by the informative work of Cooper (2009) who argues that many dyslexic learners still hide their difficulties, making it difficult to develop strategies to overcome the barriers. This type of view exists to an even greater extent in the Middle East where universities are only now just beginning to support students with dyslexia; for example in Kuwait the Australian College of Kuwait (ACK) has recently appointed a disability team to identify and support students with dyslexia and other learning disabilities (personal communication, 2010).

Issues of Accessibility and Reasonable Adjustments

Accessibility is the overriding issue. Being dyslexic can make one very vulnerable and essentially at the peril of institutional policy, which is why international research studies on sharing best practice is so essential. The ATHEN Survey on Accessible Technology in Higher Education (Asuncion, Draffan, Guinan., Thomson, (2008) is an example of this. The team collected information from colleges and universities in the United States, United Kingdom, Canada, Republic of Ireland, South Africa, Australia and New Zealand. They highlighted a wealth of useful data on the use and accessibility of technology in universities and colleges in these countries.

They found that most respondents from these countries checked at least one product in the product categories "screen readers", "screen magnification software", and "scanning/reading solutions". They did however find that there were differences among products designed for students with dyslexia in different countries. In the UK and Ireland, the "text-to-speech software applications" and "scanning/reading solutions" categories were dominated by products from the Northern Ireland based Texthelp Systems (100% of respondents in Ireland and nearly 90% in the UK reported installing and supporting TextHelp Read & Write). In contrast, the preferred scanning/reading solution in the U.S. and Canada was Kurzweil 3000 (installed and supported by 85% of U.S. and 83% of Canadian respondents).

In the UK, institutions are required by the Disability Discrimination Act to ensure that "reasonable adjustments" are made and these should be pro-active and made "in anticipation" that students with disabilities will matriculate for courses. This means that the course is deemed accessible for students with dyslexia. The findings from the Asuncion et al study (2008) wwere that accessibility seemed stronger in the UK than elsewhere, and they argue that this highlights the strength of the legal requirements in the UK. Nevertheless they do conclude their study by suggesting that there is still some way to go before there is universal access to technology-enhanced learning for students with disabilities. Technology is not the only solution to accessibility; but there is still a need to adjust to emerging technologies, and this, the authors of the study argue, will require a global effort. They urge individuals in higher education to ask questions about accessibility, both internally and externally and that vendors must be drilled about the accessibility of their products.

Identification of Need

In the UK much progress has been achieved in this area and some of the credit for this can go to the impetus of the Learning Difficulties Working Group (2005). Although they admitted that it is difficult to develop an agreed 'gold standard' of diagnostic assessment the report of the working party goes very close to achieving this.

In Canada the Ministry of Advanced Education deals with post-school provision and the necessary supports for students with Learning Disabilities (LD)[1]. They recognise that it is important to obtain uniform criteria that are practical and transparent. They emphasise that the assessment of LD is crucial. Assessors must be registered psychologists with expertise in diagnosing LD. Additionally they stress that the LD diagnosis must contain and report on the following diagnostic features:

i) Demonstration that achievement on individually administered, standardized, comprehensive tests in reading, mathematics or written expression is substantially below that expected for age, schooling and level of intelligence;

ii) That the learning disability significantly interferes with academic achievement or activities of daily living that require

---

1 In Canada and the USA the term Learning Disabilities (LD) is more commonly used rather than dyslexia. LD is broader than dyslexia and incorporates many of the categories that are included in the UK usage of the term Specific Learning Difficulties (SpLD).

reading, mathematical or writing skills. (Ministry of Advanced Education 2010).

While it is commendable to develop uniform and accountable standards we must be cautious not to equate diagnosis exclusively with testing and to ensure that accessibility is not only about technology, but about promoting effective and self sufficient learning. Assessment needs to be evidence as well as normative based.

An important factor that has impeded progress is the lack of universal agreement on what actually constitutes dyslexia. There is more agreement on the type of support students with dyslexia require than on the actual identification criteria! An interesting perspective on this is raised by the study by Anastasiou and Polychronopoulou, (2009) in Greece who analyzed identification procedures and explored the possibility of dyslexia over-identification of dyslexia in HE in Greece. Although they did not find this to be the case in Higher Education they did find a higher percentage of dyslexia in secondary education compared to primary education. They suggest that this has considerable implications for the future. They did comment that support in academic examinations was only available to students diagnosed with 'dyslexia', and not to other students with similar diagnostic labels (e.g., learning disability, reading disability, spelling disability, writing disability, dyscalculia). They argue that in terms of support, Dyslexia is the label that has the strongest currency. It is perhaps this fact that gave rise to the Greek government's concern over possible over identification of dyslexia in HE.

In the United States however, Young and Browning (2004) provide a different perspective. They show that some groups of young dyslexic adults may still be disadvantaged. Studies show that persons diagnosed with Dyslexia tend to do show only marginal differences in success compared to those with other disabilities in employment and education.

In London however, McLaughlin (2004) from the Adult Dyslexia and Skills Development Centre suggests that if dyslexic people are to be fully included in society, the emphasis should be on empowerment or enablement rather than on disability that casts the 'dyslexic as a victim'. This view is not lost to many of those who support dyslexic students at university and there is a general view that a social model needs to gain more impetus if real inclusion of those with special educational needs is to be achieved. This is the situation in the UK, Ireland and USA and Canada but the necessity for reactive on-campus support and examination accommodations is still paramount in these countries.

Most countries have made some sort of legislation attempts to support students with a recognised disability and dyslexia is recognised in terms of legislation as a disability.

In Australia and New Zealand it is only in the last few years that governments have agreed to investigate the identification of dyslexia at school level and it is likely to be some time before this has a major impact in Higher Education. Caskey (2011) cites the Reasonable Adjustments (2010) (Queensland Australia) document that attempts to highlight appropriate adjustments for students with disabilities. Some of the adjustments included for dyslexia include: readers, writers, note takers, oral examinations, modelling, additional time and help with organisation of assignments.

She also cites the Australian Disability Clearinghouse for Education and Training (ADCET) a web-based resource for support (**www.adcet.edu.au**) which provides information on teaching strategies, publications, legislation, and definitions on all disabilities, including dyslexia, for teachers in all higher educational contexts within Australia (Australian Disability Clearinghouse for Education and Training, 2008). Caskey also cites the work of Tanner (2010) in Perth, Australia which suggests that the medical model of dyslexia, may have accounted for some of the discrimination felt by students as well as for misunderstanding and lack of knowledge of dyslexia (Caskey and Tanner 2011).

In the UK all universities provide guidance for students with dyslexia and even for those who suspect they might have dyslexia, but have not yet been diagnosed. This guidance can normally be accessed from the university web page. It is perhaps the internet and international conventions and research groups rather than institutional policy that can lead the way to pursuit of equality in HE internationally for all students with dyslexia.

References

Anastasiou, D; Polychronopoulou, S, (2009) Identification and over identification of specific learning disabilities (dyslexia) in Greece. Learning Disability Quarterly March2009.

Asuncion, J., Draffan, E.A., Guinan, E.P., Thomson, T. (2008) International

Comparison on Accessible Technology in Higher Education (ATHEN) **http://athenpro.org/node/120** accessed October 2011

Australian Disability Clearinghouse for Education and Training. (2008) - Dyslexia. **http://www.adcet.gov.edu.au/ dyslexiaresourse/**

Caskey, J. (2011) Development of a Support for Learning: A Framework for Technical and Further Education (TAFE) Students with Dyslexia in Queensland. Submitted paper.

Caskey, J. (2010) personal communication

Caskey, J. And Tanner, K. (2011) Vocational Education and Training (VET Administration): Teachers' knowledge and understanding of the VET policy guidelines and teaching students with dyslexia. Paper presented at No Frills Conference Queensland Australia (2011).

Cooper, R. (2009) 'Dyslexia', in Pollak, D. (ed.) Neurodiversity in Higher

Education: Positive Responses to Specific Learning Differences, Wiley, Blackwell, Chichester, UK

Sp.LD Working Group DfES Guidlines (2005) Assessment of Dyslexia, Dyspraxia, Dyscalculia and Attention Deficit Disorder (ADD) in Higher Education. PATOSS, UK.

Tanner, K. (2010). The Lived Experience of Adults with Dyslexia: An Exploration of the Perceptions of Their Educational Experiences. Unpublished Doctor of Philosophy, Murdoch University, Perth.

Queensland VET Development Center. (2010). Reasonable Adjustment in

Teaching, Learning and Assessment for Learners' with a Disability - A Guide for

VET Practitioners. Brisbane: Department of Education and Training Qld. Australia

Dr. Gavin Reid is an international author, consultant and independent educational psycologist **www.drgavinreid.com**

THE EUROPEAN DYSLEXIA ASSOCIATION - International Organisation for Specific Learning Disabilities AISBL*

Michael Kalmár

NO MATTER WHICH COUNTRY –
NO MATTER WHICH LANGUAGE –
DYSLEXIA IS EVERYWHERE

The European Dyslexia Association is a European non-governmental umbrella organisation for national and regional associations of people with dyslexia and other specific learning differences, parents, professionals and researchers. It was founded and formally established under Belgian law in 1987 in Brussels as an international non-profit association by representatives of ten national dyslexia associations. It is the platform and the Voice of people with dyslexia and 'Specific Learning Difficulties' in Europe.

The EDA currently has 23 regional and national Effective Members in 21 EU countries, plus Switzerland and Norway, and 14 Adherent Member organisations; in all, 37 member organisations in 24 European countries:

Austria, Belgium, Cyprus, Czech Republic, Denmark, Finland, France, Germany, Greece, Ireland, Italy, Lithuania, Luxembourg, North Cyprus, Malta, the Netherlands, Norway, Poland, Portugal, Slovenia, Spain, Sweden, Switzerland and the United Kingdom.

The EDA is a Non-Governmental Organisation (NGO) affiliated to UNESCO; a Full Member of the European Disability Forum (EDF); and has Consultative Status with the International Federation of Library Associations (IFLA).

According to substantiated scientific estimates, the group of European Citizens with dyslexia and specific learning differences encompasses between 5 and 12 percent of the population, navigating through life in a largely non-'dys' friendly world. Dyslexia is the most widespread specific learning difference, making the acquisition and use of reading, spelling and writing skills and other communication-related cultural abilities difficult. Research suggests that other learning differences such as dysphasia, dyscalculia, dyspraxia and attention deficit disorder commonly co-exist with dyslexia; these are collectively known as 'DYS'-differences .. The same individual can manifest several of these differences, as dyslexia is closely associated with dysphasia, dyspraxia and dyscalculia or attention deficit.

Co-occurrence of the 'DYS'-differences is evident:

50% of people with dyslexia are dyspraxic as well.

40% of people with dyspraxia are either dyslexic or have differences in attention.

85% of people with dysphasia are dyslexic as well

20% of people with dyslexia have differences in attention, with or without hyperactivity.

50% of hyperactive children are dyslexic

It is generally (and indisputably) known and documented that the cultural abilities of reading and writing are among the most important prerequisites in our society for individual cultural, social and economic development and success. Furthermore, across Europe, the diversity of languages and multilingual demands, socio-cultural backgrounds as well as educational opportunity, have a significant influence on the manifestation of difficulties and life-chances for children, adolescents and adults with 'DYS'differences.

Without sufficient knowledge about this area, failure in school, employment, general communication impairments and social segregation are common threats, with well-known consequences for the lives of those affected, their family members and society.

More than a century of research has enabled us to increase our understanding of how humans acquire language and literacy skills, and why people with dyslexia find the process difficult to access.

There have been significant advances in procedures that enable earlier identification of dyslexia, determine which interventions work best and then develop appropriate support for people with dyslexia in schools as well as the workplace.

Despite this, dyslexia presents concerns and challenges for millions of children and adults across Europe. These challenges require major changes for governments, policymakers and organisations to improve attitudes, legislation and positive practice in education and the workplace.

Many of the issues relating to dyslexia can be improved through raising awareness of dyslexia and what can be done to adapt to it. That is why the vision of the EDA is to ensure that "every child and adult with dyslexia has the right to access and receive appropriate support and opportunity to achieve their full potential in education, training, employment and life".

Researchers acknowledge that there are many possible causes of each single or accumulated 'DYS' difference, including genetics.

There is no relationship between a person's level of intelligence, individual effort or socio-economic position and the presence of dyslexia and /or a 'DYS' difference.

It may be caused by a combination of difficulties in the cognitive development of abilities such as phonological processing, working memory, rapid naming, sequencing and the automaticity of basic skills.

At its conferences, meetings and the yearly EDA Community Summer School in San Marino, the EDA provides a platform for the most recent scientific findings in this area, best-practice interventions in the field of education and extra-curricular development as well as the advancement of affected individuals from all parts of the European Union.

The EDA is particularly interested in supporting the creation and development of national and regional organisations for people with dyslexia across the whole of Europe.

The main aim of the EDA is to inform people, politicians, policy makers, trade and commerce unions and pressure groups in Europe about the necessity of supporting those who are dyslexic or 'DYS' in a positive way, in order to avoid negative consequences caused by inappropriate education and training, low self-esteem and under-achievement which may lead to social exclusion.

With its wide range of activities, it facilitates the exchange of information and good practice through international networking and lobbying. In partnership with its member organisations, the EDA will challenge prejudice and ignorance to ensure that people with dyslexia and 'DYS' are empowered to reach their full potential.

European 'DYS'-organisations already work together in a Europe-wide network on common targets for European Institutions. The EDA has positive experiences of working in partnership with EDF (European Disability Forum) and would encourage other 'DYS' organisations to join the EDF to enhance their influence on European Institutions.

This would facilitate exchange of information and good practice through international networking and lobbying in partnership with member organisations, governmental bodies and professionals working within the different 'dys' communities.

Of critical importance is the fact that for the part of the population with dyslexia, it is very difficult to access books and any written information in normal print/format. Effectively these individuals are reading/print impaired.

Therefore our members and beneficiaries are interested in the availability of published works in accessible formats,

such as large print, Daisy, audio and braille, which can be read and enjoyed by all visually impaired and other reading disabled persons.

The EDA is working closely with the World Blind Union and the European Blind Union, lobbying the Copyright Committee (SCCR) of the World Intellectual Property Organisation (WIPO) to formulate a Treaty on Copyright and the Visually Impaired.

The target is to ensure that every child and adult with Dyslexia, Dysphasia, Dyspraxia, Dyscalculia or Attention Deficit Disorder, etc has the right to access and receive appropriate identification, support and opportunity to achieve their full potential in education, training, employment and all aspects of life.

How we function:

The activities of the EDA are organised and directed by volunteers. A Board of Directors is elected at a General Assembly of the members, held every year. The Directors' mandate is non-remunerative. The Board meets at least three times a year.

Effective membership is restricted to non-profit making dyslexia associations only. Other organisations with a scientific or social interest in dyslexia can apply for Adherent membership. However, before acquiring Effective membership, non-profit making dyslexia associations applying for membership are accepted as Adherent members only, but after two years they can apply for Effective membership.

MISSION

The European Dyslexia Association is a European umbrella organisation for national and regional associations of people with dyslexia (and other 'DYS'-differences), parents and professionals and academic researchers. It facilitates the exchange of information and good practice through international networking and lobbying. In partnership with its member organisations, the EDA will challenge prejudice and ignorance to ensure that people with dyslexia are empowered to reach their full potential.

VISION

Every child and adult with dyslexia (and/or 'DYS'-differences) in Europe has the right to access and to receive appropriate support and opportunity to achieve their full potential in education, training, employment and life.

Website: **www.eda-info.eu**
Contact président: **m.kalmar@utanet.at**
Legal address:
c/o Bureau Felix & Felix sprl
Chaussée de Tubize 135
B-1440 Braine Le Château, Belgium

*Association Internationale Sans But Lucratif

Dyslexia International

Vincent Goetry

Introduction

Dyslexia International (D.I.) is a non-governmental organization, founded in 2000. In October 2006 it was granted 'operational relations' status with UNESCO.

Our aim is to make education free and fair in accordance with the *Universal Declaration of Human Rights* (Article 26, 'Everyone has the right to an education …'). Thus we support the policies of UNESCO for free *Education for All* and *Inclusion*. We place an emphasis on promoting equal opportunity for those who struggle with reading and writing mainly by tackling the training of teachers.

We bring together local parent groups, academic researchers and teacher-training decision makers to effect change in the way dyslexia is addressed around the world.

All our work is carried out in collaboration with a team of international experts in literacy and dyslexia, headed by a Scientific Advisory Committee composed of university professors.

World Dyslexia Forum

With the collaboration of these experts, D.I. organized the World Dyslexia Forum at UNESCO in Paris in 2010. Not intended as a conference for the general public, its primary targets were teacher trainers and education policy makers although local dyslexia support groups, agencies for special needs, researchers and people with dyslexia also attended. It aimed to raise the profile of dyslexia and to establish a platform where government leaders and authorities on dyslexia could address the problems and solutions encountered in different languages and cultures. More than 350 delegates from over 90 countries attended.

By inviting a distinguished panel of experts in the six official languages of UNESCO to report on good teaching practice, we were able to assemble expertise from theoretical and practical perspectives. These experts participated in a world survey on provisions and practices around dyslexia in Arabic, Chinese, English, French, Russian and Spanish. For more information and filmed presentations of the Forum see **www.worlddyslexiaforum.org**.

Ignorance about dyslexia is still the rule rather than the exception at the world scale. One report from Kenya mentioned that 'many countries around the world, especially in Africa, still do not recognize dyslexia as a learning difficulty and have no knowledge of it. They cannot identify the dyslexic child, and even though they may realize that the child has a problem, they do not know how to handle such a child'.

With such frequently expressed needs for teacher training and in response to the findings of leading researchers that students with specific learning difficulties can nevertheless be educated in the inclusive classroom, D.I. was further motivated to develop the online learning courses for teachers presented at the Forum and to expand an e-Campus which will be launched later in 2011.

The online learning course

Dyslexia International designed this course as 'free to the end-user' in collaboration with its panel of international experts. It is divided into three major sections: What is dyslexia, how to identify it in the classroom, and what to put in place to address the educational needs of dyslexic learners.

It is addressed to *all* teachers, not only to specialist teachers.

The course is highly interactive, with written as well as filmed testimonies of people with dyslexia and their relatives, animated diagrams illustrating the process of reading, video clips of the multisensory routines to use with dyslexic learners, and links to other relevant websites including influential reports issued this century from Belgium, France, the USA and the UK.

The course was offered free to Ministries of Education at the Forum for review and implementation in their national school systems, after making suitable linguistic and cultural adaptations to meet local requirements. In order to ensure the sustainable and thorough-going diffusion of the course, D.I. stipulated that three key local partners should be involved: decision makers in education, university researchers and local associations wherever possible.

Belgium has taken a powerful initiative in tackling the problem. The ministry has introduced the online learning course and encouraged teachers to take part in it across all five regions of francophone Belgium.

In her introductory speech at the launch of this initiative, the francophone Minister of Obligatory Education, Marie-Dominique Simonet, cited a survey conducted by associations of parents in France. The results show that 79 % of the parents who took part in the study considered that learning difficulties such as dyslexia were not well addressed by the French school system. Nevertheless, no fewer than 49 % of them considered that these learning difficulties were in fact identified by the school system. According to the Minister, this is *"a paradox which points out the need for the training of teachers"*.

Trainers taught by the course director, Vincent Goetry, in turn train teachers in Belgium with a blended scheme which will ally distance learning using the online course and in-person training, putting the teachers into the shoes of dyslexic learners, for example.

The teachers who have studied the online learning course will be in a position to act as multipliers, encouraging other staff in their school also to undertake the course.

So far, more than 30 countries in different regions of the world have manifested interest in using the course or are in the process of implementing it in their systems. Projects are underway for translations into Portuguese and Arabic. In Mali the course will be piloted in selected schools in order to adapt it to the cultural and linguistic settings of that country. The plan then is to introduce it into the initial training of teachers. In other countries, such as Ireland, the course is already being implemented together with the three key actors mentioned above.

The e-Campus

A steering committee was set up at the World Dyslexia Forum. The role of this committee was to feed discussions about setting up an e-Campus, a 'virtual' university, now under development.

The e-Campus will be a platform for free courses and resources, which will be selected by a panel of international experts in literacy and dyslexia. It will include a library with selected films, papers, books and other resources; a platform for video conferences and tutorials; a test centre with selected questionnaires and tools to assess whether a person might have dyslexia; and a laboratory describing the latest research in the neurosciences and other relevant disciplines in relationship to dyslexia.

Lobbying at UNESCO

As an NGO in operational relations with UNESCO, we are keenly aware of our responsibility – to speak for people with dyslexia across the world.

We try to participate to as many meetings on education as possible and attempt to feature in at least one public event each year in Paris.

Conclusion

Despite some changes in policy, education worldwide is still not generally free, and most teachers are not adequately trained to support students with learning difficulties.

Even in countries where education is accessible, *30 to 40 %* of children leave school with literacy levels which will not allow them to pursue further and higher education.

More specifically, one cannot ignore the fact that 10 % of the population worldwide, that is over 600 million, will experience minor to major difficulties in acquiring written language. These figures cannot be ignored when trying to tackle the problem of illiteracy.

By making teacher training the priority, Dyslexia International aims to improve education so that *all* learners can become literate.

The education world has to change.

Vincent Goetry PhD, *Consultant in Literacy and Dyslexia*

Organisations

British Dyslexia Association

Kate Saunders

What The B.D.A. Does

The B.D.A. is the voice of dyslexic people. The B.D.A. works to support dyslexic individuals across all age ranges. It seeks to bring about a dyslexic friendly society, where all dyslexic individuals can fulfil their potential.

The B.D.A. seeks to achieve the following goals:

1. Early identification of dyslexic difficulties for all in society.

2. Availability of effective and appropriate teaching provision for all dyslexic children and adults.

3. Availability of appropriate assessments for all dyslexic children and adults.

4. Availability of reasonable adjustments for dyslexic individuals within all sectors of society (including education, employment, training and the criminal justice services).

5. Information should be available for dyslexic individuals across the age ranges and sectors, and for those who support them, about effective strategies to help overcome dyslexia related difficulties, and how to maximise the strengths of those with dyslexia.

The B.D.A. champions these goals with policy makers at local and national level. B.D.A. training events spread awareness and skills to around16,000 people a year. The Helpline (0845-251-9002) receives around 20,000 calls and 6,000 emails a year. B.D.A. sets the gold standard for dyslexia specialist training; accrediting training courses for Approved Teacher Status (ATS), Approved Practitioner Status (APS) and Associate Member of the British Dyslexia Association (AMBDA) level. The B.D.A. runs educational and employer conferences, has stands and speakers at major educational exhibitions and takes an active part in consultations with government about dyslexia related policy issues.

There are 71 Local Dyslexia Associations affiliated to the B.D.A. and these collectively are supported by around 500 volunteers. The Local Associations generally offer support through a range of events. Some also have local helplines and may offer wider services (e.g. tutoring/workshops, screening and assessments). Schools, other educational establishments, companies and organisations also support the B.D.A. by becoming Organisational Members

(please see **www.bdadyslexia.org.uk/membership.html** tel: 01344-381563).

The B.D.A. sets the standard for what a school, college, university or organisation should do if it is to be dyslexia friendly. The B.D.A. assists organisations to achieve a set of dyslexia friendly criteria leading, if successful, to the award of the B.D.A. Dyslexia Friendly Quality Mark

(please see **www.bdadyslexia.org.uk/quality-mark-and-accreditation.html**, tel: 01344-38-1551 for more details).

The full range of the activities undertaken by the B.D.A. are shown in the diagram below:

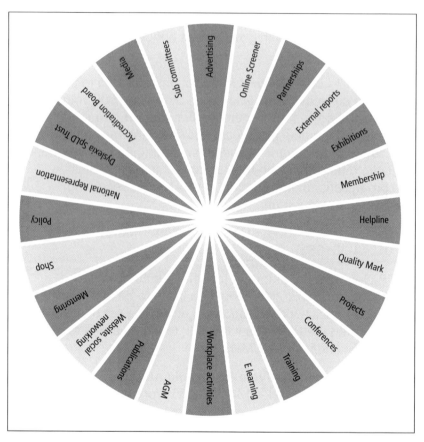

Acknowledging the potential strengths of dyslexic individuals is crucial. Being dyslexic can be extremely frustrating and challenging, and the B.D.A. respects the tremendous determination, hard work, positive skills, ingenuity, creativity, problem solving and verbal interaction skills that dyslexics often demonstrate when of tackling their difficulties. The tremendous privilege of working with, and in support of, dyslexic individuals is the witnessing of these attributes.

The generous help of B.D.A. supporters assisting through fundraising, legacies and volunteering enable B.D.A. to continue working towards the goal of creating a dyslexia friendly world.

SpLD Trust

Mel Byrne and Dr. John Rack

The Dyslexia-SpLD Trust is a collaboration of voluntary and community organisations involved in promoting improved practice and outcomes for children with dyslexia and specific learning difficulties. Our founding organisations are The British Dyslexia Association, Dyslexia Action, Helen Arkell Dyslexia Centre, Springboard for Children, Patoss and Xtraordinary People.

What we do

- Advise and liaise directly with government.
- Inform, advise and signpost parents, teachers and local authorities about training, interventions and research.
- Bring together those organisations committed to improving the lives of dyslexic individuals.
- Support organisations to upscale and roll out examples of best practice that improve outcomes for children and young people with dyslexia.

Why is our work important?

- We offer one platform for the government and stakeholders to engage with.
- We improve choice for parents, teachers and local authorities by having a wide ranging knowledge.
- We provide reliable information by working with experts in the field.
- Add value to specialist services by having an overview of the wider SEN picture through our engagement with Autism Education Trust (AET), The Communications Trust (TCT) and the strategic partners.

Key Achievements

- A Professional Development Framework
- Interventions for Literacy navigation site for parents and teachers

Our work with parents and stakeholders is our focus over the next two years. We welcome all views.

For further details visit: **www.thedyslexia-SpLDtrust.org.uk**

Dyslexia Action

Dyslexia Action is a national charity and provider of services and support for people with dyslexia and literacy difficulties. Its services are offered through 26 Centres and additional outposts around the country.

The educational charity offers assessments, specialist tuition, courses for learners and parents, awareness talks, workplace and educational institution consultancy and teacher training. It also gives free advice and supplies dyslexia support materials for teachers, psychologists, parents and learners.

Services and support are provided to children, adults, parents, educational institutions and employers. The dyslexia and specific learning difficulties training is available to teachers and teaching assistants.

Helen Arkell Dyslexia Centre

Bernadette McLean

April 2011 was our 40th anniversary which was celebrated at our annual golf day.

The demand for assessments continues to grow and our team of assessors expands annually.

With the new regulatory requirement for continuing professional development we offer a range of courses so that our graduates can maintain their practising certificates up to date.

Professional training ranges from foundation to Masters Level.

Government funding for training has come to an end but we will continue to offer low-cost training for TA's on dyslexia and co-occurring attention deficit disorder and dyscalculia

Our Saturday morning conferences are proving popular and details of these and all other servicescan be found on our website. **www.arkellcentre.org.uk**

Patoss– The Professional Association of Teachers of Students with Specific Learning Difficulties

Lynn Greenwold

Patoss is for all those concerned with the teaching and support of pupils with dyslexia and specific learning difficulties.

Patoss promotes good practice amongst professionals and has guidelines for those moving into this field as well as for parents and established practitioners.

Patoss maintains a list of SpLD professionals providing services as assessors and tutors. We respond to thousands of requests every year putting parents, students and disability advisors in touch with our professional members.

Patoss offers:

- Practising certificates to underpin professional standards,
- CPD opportunities to help assessors and teachers maintain the highest standards in their fields
- A range ofinsurance including professional indemnity
- and much more.

Visit the Patoss website: **www.patoss-dyslexia.org**

Adult Dyslexia Organisation

Donald Schloss

ADO is the national organisation for adult dyslexics, run by dyslexics for dyslexics, providing a wide range of services to the public and professionals, service providers and policy makers.

By working with government departments, major organisations, Trade Unions, educators and employers, ADO ensures real change that affects the lives of adults with dyslexia.

ADO has now been established for over 20 years and continues to support and develop support groups within the community, the workplace and educational institutions.

ADO represents adult dyslexics on a number of government committees and consultations, and believes by working together things can improve.

Contact Details:

Donald Schloss

Chief Executive

Adult Dyslexia Organisation (ADO)

Ground Floor, Secker House, Minet Road, Loughborough Estate, London, SW9 7TP

Admin: 020-7207-3911 Mobile 0797-4-755163

E-mail: **ado.dns@dial.pipex.com**

The Association of Dyslexia Specialists in Higher Education (ADSHE)

ADSHE was established in 2001 to share knowledge and inform good practice. It is the professional body for support specialists working with students with dyslexia, dyspraxia and other SpLDs in Higher Education, whether in universities or FE colleges.

ADSHE provides continuing professional development events and there are eleven regional groups which provide training and valuable networking opportunities for tutors who may be working in isolation or very small groups.

ADSHE Jiscmail is an essential point of contact with other specialists providing up to date information on national issues, new developments in research, screening and assessment, teaching methods and other relevant issues.

www.adshe.org.uk

Dyslexia Scotland

Cathy Magee

Dyslexia Scotland aims to encourage and enable children, young people and adults with dyslexia to reach their potential in education, employment and life. Based in Stirling, our network of volunteer-led local branches (currently 15 and growing) across Scotland offers support at a grassroots level.

Our 3 key aims are set out in our current Strategic Plan:

Offering high quality services at national and local levels

Influencing national positive change

Supporting and sustaining our network of branches, members and volunteers.

Key highlights in 2010/11 include:

- 3 new volunteer-led branches in our network
- Wide dissemination in Scotland, as well as internationally, of the comprehensive free online 'Assessing Dyslexia' toolkit launched in June 2010. **http://www.frameworkforinclusion. org/AssessingDyslexia/**
- Exciting partnerships to influence dyslexia-friendly workplace support – including a Dyslexia Guide launched by the Scottish Trade Unions Congress for union learning representatives; delivery of our first corporate membership package for NHS Education for Scotland
- Plans to develop a DVD with the Scottish Prison Service to encourage prisoners with dyslexia to take up learning opportunities

For further details contact:

Dyslexia Scotland, Stirling Business Centre,
Wellgreen, Stirling, FK8 2DZ.

Email: **info@dyslexiascotland.org.uk**
Website: **www.dyslexiascotland.org.uk**

Telephone: 01786-44-6650
Dyslexia Scotland Helpline: 0844-800-8484

Cathy Magee is Chief Executive of Dyslexia Scotland

Dyslecsia Cymru / Wales Dyslexia

A charity based in Wales founded in 2001 and now in partnership with University of Wales Trinity St David, aiming to address the needs of dyslexic individuals of all ages in a bilingual nation. Since devolution the educational system in Wales has increasingly diverged from that in England; reflecting this divergence are the conversion of the DST-J into the Welsh language, the production of a Welsh language speech to text programme and the existence of a bilingual help line. Courses at a variety of levels are currently under development in collaboration with Trinity St David.

Dyslecsia Cymru/Wales Dyslexia
University of Wales Trinity St David
Carmarthen
SA31 3EP
01267-676629
www.walesdyslexia.co.uk

The Arts Dyslexia Trust

This non-profit making Trust has been set up with the following aims:

- To help to bridge the gulf of misunderstanding that seems too often to exist between those who think predominantly in verbal terms and those who think in predominantly visual-spatial terms.

- To draw attention to the high creative potential of the many visually-dominant dyslexic minds.

- To encourage, instigate, and engage in research into the cause and nature of this connection between dyslexia and good visual-spatial faculties which can lead to exceptional ability and achievement in the arts and sciences (most noticeably, perhaps, in the visual arts).

- To provide an advisory service for all those concerned with the above questions, most particularly in the field of education. The Trust also offers practical help to students and adults in their training and careers.

- To persuade more people wherever they live in the world to appreciate the importance of visual-spatial thinking in every creative activity (in the visual arts and other areas as well), and to use their own visual-spatial thinking capacity more effectively. This ability to think in visual terms is a valuable specific attribute of the human brain which we all possess to a greater or lesser extent according to our individual genetic make-up. We want to encourage everyone to recognize and develop it both for their own practical purposes and enjoyment, and also for the greater understanding of the world we live in and of our relationship to it, so that new ways towards solving the many problems that face us all may be found.

SpLD Assessment Standards Committee [SASC]

SASC is a standard-setting group concerned with the diagnostic assessment of specific learning difficulties in an educational setting. SASC seeks to extend the principles of good practice across all age ranges and throughout the profession.

SASC runs a CPD authorisation scheme for specialist teachers and other professionals engaged in the diagnostic assessment of SpLDs.

From March 2012 a minimum of 5 hours CPD for holders of Assessment Practising Certificates must be delivered by SASC Authorised Providers. See SASC website for listing.

SASC aims to

- promote and monitor standards of SpLD assessor training relating to all age ranges
- promote and monitor standards of CPD in SpLD assessment
- oversee and approve processes of awarding SpLD Assessment Practising Certificates & maintain a list of approved evaluators for APL/APE applications

Website: **www.sasc.org.uk**
e-mail: **info@sasc.org.uk**

The Miles Dyslexia Centre / Canolfan Dyslexia Miles, Bangor University

Dr Markéta Caravolas

Research: Director Dr Markéta Caravolas is leading six projects investigating literacy development and dyslexia in several European languages. We are also studying early reading and spelling development in Welsh-English bilingual children with the aim of creating new language-sensitive tests. In partnership with Remploy, a project is underway developing assessment tools to help adults access and maintain employment.

Our Student Service contributes to Bangor's drive to develop an inclusive learning environment and is involved in initiatives concerning adult dyslexia and employment.

Assessment Service: Educational Psychologists work with children and adults; our Higher Education Assessment and Reporting Team (HEARTS) assesses HE students, while STARs assessors (Specialist Teacher Assessment and Reporting) work with the 11-18 age group. We provide consultations on appropriate assessment and support.

With LEAs referring fewer children for specialist help, our Teaching Service now meets increased demand for school INSET training, and after-school and private teaching.

We run Training Courses (B.D.A.-accredited) for teachers and LSAs

see: **www.dyslexia.bangor.ac.uk**

CReSTeD (the Council for the Registration of Schools Teaching Dyslexic pupils)

CReSTeD is a registered charity established in 1996. Its purpose is to help parents and those who advise them choose appropriate schools for children with specific learning difficulties.

CReSTeD schools are visited every three years by a CReSTeD consultant to review the quality of the schools' provision for SpLD. A satisfactory visit leads to an entry on the CReSTeD register, where schools are categorised according to the type of provision offered. CReSTeD works with Dyslexia Action and the B.D.A. to provide parents with an authorative source of schools with high quality provision.

CReSTeD can be contacted through its Administrator, Mrs Lesley Farrer at Old Post House, Castle Street, Whittington, Shropshire, SY11 4DF. Telephone: 01691-655783/0845-601-5013. Email: **lesley@crested.org.uk**

Dyslexia Association of Ireland

Founded in 1972, the Dyslexia Association of Ireland (DAI) works to educate people in Ireland about dyslexia, and also offers appropriate assessment and effective dyslexia support services for children and adults . The Association has 3000 member families, and a network of 34 affiliated branches nationwide, offering local community-based services.

Services offered by DAI include:

- Information.
- Assessment/diagnosis.
- Specialist tuition for children and adults, including a unique full-time course for unemployed adults with dyslexia.
- Courses for parents.
- Training for teachers and other education personnel.
- Dyslexia awareness training.
- Lobbying and advocacy.

For further information, please contact DAI at:

Address: Suffolk Chambers,
1 Suffolk Street, Dublin 2, Ireland.
Telephone: 01-6790-276

Email: **info@dyslexia.ie**
Website: **www.dyslexia.ie**

Committees

National Technology Committee

Di Hillage

The various members of the NTC have continued to support the B.D.A. by helping on the stand at exhibitions, by giving seminars at BETT and the Education Show and by working to support dyslexic people in their various careers and local activities.

Our main progress of late has been the creation of our own website at **www.bdatech.org**. This enables us to provide information on a wide range of topics relating to dyslexia and the ways in which modern technology can offer support. Thanks to the efforts of Judith Stansfield, Cheryl Dobbs and Jean Hutchins, this enables us to provide information and keep it up to date much more easily than before. We also have our own email contact at **bdatech@btinternet.com** for anyone wishing to ask specific questions.

Sadly for us, Cheryl will be returning to Australia soon. We thank her for all her efforts on behalf of the committee. We hope she will remain in contact as an associate member and look forward to hearing news of related issues 'down under'.

The report on the Accessible Resources Pilot Project, in which EA Draffan was heavily involved, was published and can be found at **http://www.altformat.org/mytextbook/**. This suggests that some dyslexic learners have become disaffected by their inability to read school textbooks and that modern technology can do much to help overcome this problems. Hopefully this message will soon begin to reach schools. Meanwhile those in Scotland have recognised the financial benefits of using technology to replace readers and scribes in exam and are now providing digital versions of the papers.

Jean Hutchins continues her indefatigable campaign to make sure that alternative formats of published materials are available and that the various packages which provide text to speech facilities do so in a convenient way. She also oversees the annual production of the B.D.A. disc, which has sample programs from several supporting companies, together with loads of other information. The disc is then available as a free handout at exhibitions and other events.

The impact of smart mobile technology is considerable nowadays and we are keen to hear of apps for such devices that dyslexic users have found useful.

Despite such developments we still hear of incidences where dyslexic youngsters, particularly those of school age, are made to feel inferior to their peers when technology to help them is not being made available. This is in spite of the considerable investment in computer technology that has been made by the schools concerned. Concern for internet safety and security seems to override all other considerations, despite the results of projects such as the one mentioned above and the Home Access Project, which showed that youngsters did not abuse the facilities they were given.

Those who overcome their difficulties sufficiently to reach University are given resources under the Disabled Students' Allowance scheme. Would it not make sense to provide such support earlier in their years of education? The media is full of complaints about school leavers' inadequate literacy skills, yet none seems to have made this rather obvious suggestion to help raise standards.

Music Committee Article 2011

Sheila Oglethorpe

This has been a busy year for the Music Committee, starting with the seminar "Music Teaching and Dyslexia: Practical Insights" that we put on at The Abbey Centre, Westminster in February.

It was a lively occasion with lots of interaction between the participants and a very friendly atmosphere, perhaps because we were all seated at round tables in cabaret style so that we were in manageable groups. One member of the committee was allotted to each table and we had prepared a list of things that we thought might encourage the delegates to get going talking to each other, such as: "How does one find out the way one's pupil learns best?" or "How does dyslexia affect the teaching of music theory? What are the differences between the approaches to this and the practical side of music?" On some tables we hardly needed the list at all!

We were a little disappointed that there weren't quite as many people there as we had hoped for, but there were certainly enough and it did mean that for those of our speakers who wanted actively to involve the whole audience, there was enough space. We had all advertised it as much as possible, but obviously there are limits to what people are prepared to come to towards the end of February. We are learning. It was extremely successful nonetheless and we had some very enthusiastic comments afterwards.

The morning started off with an authoritative, clear and helpful explanation of what the latest findings on dyslexia are, given by Kate Saunders. This was followed by a stimulating workshop given by Katie Overy, incorporating some of her latest research on Rhythm Games for Literacy Support, which gave us all an opportunity to walk about and dance around. Following the tea break, two other members of our committee, Paula Bishop-Liebler and Karen Marshall, assisted by Andy Fell from the

B.D.A. Assistive Technology Committee, gave us an insight into how we could use technology in our teaching of dyslexics. This is an area which is expanding all the time so it was very helpful to be brought up to date, particularly for those of us who teach in the classroom.

Following a sandwich lunch and a lot of networking, we were initiated into the wonders of the Kodaly approach to learning music by Cyrilla Rowsell. Many of us had not had the opportunity to partake in a Kodaly workshop before and seemed to know very little about it. Cyrilla put us in the learning situation, which some found quite challenging, but it was easy to sit out and others less shy thoroughly enjoyed it and gave good entertainment to the audience!

This in turn was followed by a hands-on approach to Dyslexia, Music and the Dalcroze method given by Jacqueline Vann, who had brought along lots of colourful balls and ribbons and scarves. This reminded us how colour can enliven a situation and it provided a wonderful conclusion to the events at which we had all learnt such a lot.

Committee work is, of course, ongoing all the time and once the seminar was over, we turned our attention to strengthening the ties that we already have with the Associated Board of the Royal Schools of Music. They have been supportive for many years, being the first examination board to make provisions for dyslexic candidates. Some of our members have also been lecturing on the AB Certificate of Teaching course year by year since 1996. This has been a fruitful experience and has actually resulted in the presence of one participant on the course now being one of our committee. There is another participant we are keeping an acquisitive eye on, who is at present doing a PhD on the subject of music and dyslexia, having decided to find out more after a talk by a committee member.

The Chief Executive of the ABRSM, with two of his colleagues, met with three of us from the committee in June to hear of our ideas for a closer collaboration. We were very warmly received and are looking forward to more invitations to spread the word at some of the AB events. There is no doubt about their willingness to be of the utmost assistance to dyslexics.

Another idea that we are considering at the moment, for widening the number of people involved and interested in music and dyslexia, is to set up a Google or Moodle group. We are about to produce a mini-guide to dyslexia and music teaching which can be downloaded free of charge from the Internet. All our members have contributed to this and we have had strict instructions to keep it short, precise and readable in the modern style with plenty of bullet points! The mini-guide will be advertised in the November/December bulletin from the B.D.A..

Meanwhile, we continue to get a little stream of requests or queries through the B.D.A. helpline which need attention. Some of these can be answered by giving information about the books we have published, but we have recently had a cry for help from a university student who was only diagnosed as having dyslexia at the start of her course. She is now approaching the end and she still needs to pass her Grade 5 theory exam. She also finds memorising very hard and has set herself the task of completing her final performance by performing from memory. The courage and determination of some dyslexics is most humbling. Two of our members are going to do their best to help. This sounds important.

Possibly less importantly, but we take every request seriously, there has been a request for information about reading music with coloured bar lines that had been mentioned in a GMTV programme. I am afraid that none of our members had heard of it or seen the programme. Perhaps they were all too busy playing music! Is there anyone out there who can advise us??

The Dyscalculia Group

Steve Chinn

The B.D.A. is planning to set up a subcommittee on dyscalculia, a specific learning difficulty with arithmetic and mathematics. There are some good reasons as to why this is an opportune time to take this initiative.

Dyscalculia is a relatively new word in the vocabulary of education, even though it has been used in research for over 40 years. The quantity of research into dyscalculia is still quite small in comparison to that into dyslexia and thus our understanding of this issue is in its infancy. We do know that it often co-occurs alongside dyslexia and we know that neither is attributable to the other even though there are several characteristics shared by both.

Professor Brian Butterworth, a world renowned researcher into dyscalculia will be working with the group. Steve Chinn has agreed to Chair the group and has asked Pete Jarrett, a specialist in the tertiary sector and Jill Higginson, a specialist teacher in the SENSS team at Staffordshire County Council to join the group. We are currently canvassing to find a dyscalculic adult to join the group.

Our first meeting will be in November 2011 and we will be setting up our aims, discussing some key issues and setting priorities for our first year. Among the topics we need to consider for inclusion in our priorities are:

Raising awareness of dyscalculia and how it can be identified and addressed in schools and in FE and HE; how it should be distinguished from dyslexia.

Providing succinct and pragmatic information and advice

Seeking international links and information on training, encouraging research, advocacy in education, employment and training and setting up a list of tutors.

B.D.A. Accreditation for Dyslexia Specialist Teachers

Mike Johnson

The B.D.A. Accreditation Board accredits specialist Dyslexia Teacher Courses Nationally and Internationally. At the start of his second report, "Identifying and Teaching Children and Young People with Dyslexia and Literacy Difficulties" (Rose, J, 2009) Sir Jim Rose makes the following statements:

> "Reading disorders have been extensively researched such that dyslexia, the existence of which was once questioned, is now widely recognised as a specific difficulty in learning to read. Research also shows that dyslexia may affect more than the ability to read and write. (p.2)
>
> Secondly, the long running debate about its existence should give way to building professional expertise in identifying dyslexia and developing effective ways to help learners overcome its effects. (p.9)"

February this year saw the 25th anniversary of the earliest awards of Associate Membership of the British Dyslexia Association (AMBDA) given in 1986 following courses provided by the then Dyslexia Institute and the Helen Arkell Dyslexia Centre. Courses leading to the awards of Approved Teacher Status (ATS) and AMBDA are now seen as the 'Gold Standard' for developing such specialist professional expertise. Around 2,500 places on ATS and AMBDA courses were fully funded by the Teacher Development Agency in 2010-11 and holders of AMBDA are eligible to apply for award of an Assessment Practising Certificate, allowing its holders to perform formal assessments for Dyslexia/Specific Learning Difficulties (SpLD) and subsequent concessions, previously the province of only educational psychologists. The only trained teacher needed for the new 'Free Schools' is one with a specialist qualification for the teaching of pupils with SEN. A course leading to AMBDA would seem most appropriate. We have come a long way in 25 years.

The B.D.A. now has a full set of awards offering a complete career progression for educational professionals working with pupils having difficulties with literacy. For Teaching Assistants this progression begins with Accredited Learning Support Assistant (ALSA). This is normally offered by a Local Authority with support and validation from a college or university. It focuses on working with teachers with understanding and practical skills. It can be followed by entry to the new Approved Practitioner Status (APS) award. The criteria for this award are the same as for Approved Teacher Status (ATS) and courses are co-taught but APS is awarded to those without UK qualified teacher status (QTS). This is particularly important given the significant proportion of pupils with SEN being supported by teaching assistants and support assistants now have a clear specialist career progression.

ATS is recognised by the Teacher Development Agency (TDA) as the basic qualification for a specialist dyslexia/SpLD teacher. Those holding the award (and APS) have a critical understanding of the nature and causes of dyslexia and are competent in both informal, curriculum-based assessment and the delivery of appropriate specialist teaching.

The final award is AMBDA for which QTS (or certain other professional qualifications) is an essential pre-requisite. Holders of AMBDA have a deep, critical understanding of the theories and research underpinning contemporary understanding of the nature, causes and effects of dyslexia and its assessment, They are competent in the use of both informal and psychometrically based tests and can apply for a Dyslexia/SpLD Assessment Practising Certificate enabling them to undertake formal assessment of and reporting on learners thought to have dyslexic type difficulties. Both ATS and AMBDA have specialist variations for those working in further or higher education.

In addition the B.D.A. also accredits **AMBDA Numeracy, a course** designed for those working with dyslexic learners in the mathematics classroom.

B.D.A. accredited courses must be validated by Higher Education Institutions to ensure that the highest possible standards are maintained. Full details are on the B.D.A. web site **http://www.bdadyslexia.org.uk**

Through an appointed Liaison Team courses leading to a B.D.A. award are scrutinised by the Accreditation Board composed of a balance of Course Leaders, Local Authority Representatives, Academics and Researchers from the field of dyslexia.

Increasingly in recent years the Board has been receiving proposals from outside the UK. There are currently courses in Greece, Malta and Kuwait. The latest proposals are from South Africa and Singapore. These courses fulfil the same criteria as those in the UK but also demonstrate how they take into consideration the cultural and linguistic context in which they are delivered. The Kuwait and Singapore courses are currently considering delivery in the 'home' language. In response to this increasing demand, the B.D.A. has recently launched an International Accreditation Board.

B.D.A. courses emphasise *critical* understanding of the causes and manifestations of dyslexia and of the principles underlying methods proposed for specialist intervention. B.D.A. awards require course participants to demonstrate the ability to deliver and monitor structured, sequential, phonics-based multi-sensory teaching methods. For ATS / APS and AMBDA they must also demonstrate an ability to assess learners felt to be demonstrating dyslexic type difficulties. An understanding of dyslexia friendly classroom teaching methods and the effects of dyslexia that go beyond difficulty with literacy skills is also required. The B.D.A. recognises that there are several schemes and methods that lay more emphasis in one or more of these areas and that multi-sensory instruction does not help all learners with dyslexic type difficulties. However, they feel that it is important for specialist teachers to have a firm, confident basis to begin their specialist teaching and on which to consider critically alternative methods. Similarly, the Board is not dogmatic about the way in which courses develop their courses to meet the criteria. The two members of the Board who comprise a course Liaison Team see their role as a collaborative one as 'critical friends' in the development of a course that meets the relevant criteria.

B.D.A. awards require their holders to submit a Continuing Professional Development (CPD) Portfolio every three years detailing the Professional Development Activities and direct teaching they have undertaken so as to remain conversant with knowledge, skills and professional competence required of them in their specialist teaching role.

The usual route to a B.D.A. award is through an accredited course. However, it is possible to seek accreditation through Individual Merit by presenting evidence of an ability to fulfil both the course content criteria and successful teaching of appropriate learners using structured, sequential, phonics-based multi-sensory methods.

At the heart of the accreditation of both individuals and courses lies the Accreditation Board. This meets three times a year and its members scrutinise all proposals for accreditation and four-yearly re-accreditation of courses, all requests for accreditation by individuals and all CPD Portfolios. They also consider the impact of any relevant developments in the field in relation to course content and criteria particularly that resulting from the work of the Liaison Teams. To say the meetings are lively is an understatement.

The latest developments are firstly the recognition of the B.D.A. by the SpLD Assessment Standards Committee (SASC) as one of the three awarding bodies for the SpLD Assessment Practising Certificate. Schools, colleges and parents will now no longer have to seek the services of an educational psychologist to determine the appropriate specialist intervention for a learner thought to have dyslexia. They can do this either by fulfilling the Rose recommendation that:

"Schools should ensure either that at least one of their teachers has, or obtains this level of expertise (ATS for informal, curriculum-based assessment, AMBDA for formal reporting)

or

that they have good access to such a teacher through partnership arrangements with other schools." (page 18)

The B.D.A. Accreditation Board will continue the important work of setting and maintaining the gold standard for dyslexia/SpLD teaching and assessment training and qualifications.

Secondly:

"The DCSF should ask the Training Development Agency for Schools and the initial teacher training sector to build on initiatives for strengthening coverage of special educational needs and disability (including dyslexia) in initial teacher training courses."

The B.D.A. has been proactive in this regard. At the Manchester Metropolitan University (MMU) the ITT course offers, students the ability to gain the award of ATS (ITT) through the Optional Course structure in Years 3 and 4. Following submission of evidence of appropriate professional development in their first two years of teaching this can be converted to 'full' ATS and, following an appropriate in-service course, AMBDA. All universities offering ITT will be circulated with the details of criteria leading to ATS (ITT) in the Autumn and offered support to incorporate this opportunity for their students from the member of the Accreditation Board from MMU.

It has been said that one should never make predictions, particularly about the future. However, we are clear during the next 25 years the B.D.A. will continue to strive to ensure that any learner with dyslexia will have access to an appropriately qualified specialist teacher as soon as possible.

Any communication in relation to Accreditation, please send directly or copy to **accreditation@bdadyslexia.org.uk**

Leicestershire Dyslexia Association

Chris Hossack

The Leicestershire Dyslexia Association was originally called the 'Dyslexia Support Group Leicestershire' and it was formed by a group of parents coming together after an appeal was made on Radio Leicester by a lady called Rosemarie Christian. Rosemarie had a dyslexic son called Ben and she wanted to know if there were any other parents out there who were having similar problems with their dyslexic children and if any of them would be interested in forming a support group for families.

The first meeting was held in June 1984 and the Support Group was set up during the following year, 1985, and then became affiliated to the British Dyslexia Association. The name was changed to the Leicestershire Dyslexia Association in 1994 to bring it in line with other local Dyslexia Associations, but the group still retains the same ethos of self-help that it had at the beginning.

Our current membership is about 100, made up mostly of parents and teachers. We work closely with other local groups including Dyslexia Action, Patoss and the Dyspraxia Foundation. We provide open meetings at least once a term, one of which includes a national speaker such as Professor Maggie Snowling, Dr Tilly Mortimore, Philomena Ott and Ruth Miskin. At these events we usually invite either SEN Marketing to provide a book display, or software providers to show their latest products.

We have helpliners strategically placed in Market Harborough, Loughborough and Melton Mowbray, as well as in Leicester. They answer phone calls and e mails through the website from worried parents, schools, adult dyslexics and those in the caring professions, on a host of different topics at all hours of the day and night. Having that local information about schools and agencies in the neighbourhood is a huge advantage, as well as being able to relate to local situations.

We have a good working relationship with Children and Young People's Services, both in the city as well as the county, and we are represented on their forums relating to dyslexic friendly schools, on which they are making excellent progress. This also enables us to feed back both good and bad news when necessary. We have been delighted to work with them, organising conferences, drop-ins and sharing special events during |Dyslexia Awareness Week. We are in close contact with the Special Needs Teaching Teams, and have shared open days and road shows around the city and county with them.

The Teaching Workshop was set up in 1989 by two specialist teachers. The aim of the workshop was to give dyslexic young people help with their reading and spelling, but also to help them to develop coping strategies and discover their strengths so that they could use these to overcome their difficulties.

The Saturday Workshop started with just 3 pupils, which quickly increased to 10 and by 1992 we had a waiting list, but we were short of space in our premises at the Woodgate Resource Centre. We had also acquired our first computer with some funding from the Health Authority and needed a dedicated room to leave it set up. So in 1992 we moved to the hall at the back of Stoneygate Baptist Church and set up our first computer room. Since then, we have taken over 2 other rooms off the hall as a second computer room and a resource centre and photocopier location, and we use several other rooms in the church buildings as teaching rooms.

The number of young people is now about 30 and the number of teachers and helpers has grown to about 15. Some of our computer room staff have grown up with us, having attended workshop as students, and have now become helpers. The group is run as a co-operative, parents paying basic fees and teachers and helpers receiving expenses only. The balance of income goes towards a very fair rental on the hall, as well as towards buying equipment and materials. We are very grateful to members of Stoneygate Baptist Church for their continued support of our work.

Being in touch with a constantly changing group of parents does mean that we are able to bring new talents to our committee, who run the association entirely on a voluntary basis. Fund raising has included a sponsored bike ride round Rutland Water, sponsored swims, the most recent of which was undertaken by one of our parents as Team Gorey(see Fundraise/Fundraising Stories on the B.D.A. website). The slightly less energetic provision of a tuck shop at workshop with the recent introduction of bacon cobs has proved a real earner!!

For many years we worked with the University of Leicester in providing conferences of national significance. We are now involved with supporting the AMBDA courses, run jointly with the Special Needs Teaching Service of the city, which have grown significantly through being part funded following the Rose Report recommendations.

As an Association, we have always been keen to support the B.D.A. in whatever ways we can. A number of parents have helped on the B.D.A. stand at the Education Show in Birmingham, an experience they found really exciting in realising how much they have learnt about dyslexia in coming to meetings and chatting at workshop with other parents and teachers. One young man who has worked with us for some years is now on the staff of B.D.A. and another comes regularly to Special Needs London to help on the stand there. We have been pleased to host the Members Day last year,as well as providing a location for national training courses and B.D.A. meetings.

We are confident of continuing for years ahead, for although more and more information is available on the various websites, being able to speak to someone who understands where you are coming from makes resolving the issue so much easier. From the early days of the association, when we were frankly at loggerheads with schools and the authority in getting dyslexia recognised, things have moved on dramatically so that we now have a good working relationship towards helping that 10% of the population with dyslexia.

Friends of the B.D.A.

Kate Saunders

The 'Friends of the B.D.A.' are a group of volunteers who kindly offer their time and services to support the B.D.A..

Each individual brings their own set of skills, experience and interests, which can then be matched with the volunteering requirements of the B.D.A. nationally and locally. This may include organising fundraising events, supporting campaign issues, promoting awareness about dyslexia in all sectors of society and coming together at events and exhibitions to strengthen the B.D.A. presence.

The B.D.A. is seeking to expand this group. If you have the time and energy to give to support this drive we want to hear from you! Please get in contact with Eorann Lean. Personal Assistant to the Chief Executive Officer, **admin@bdadyslexia.org.uk** 01344-381551

There is much work to be done to ensure that all areas of education, employment and services are fully aware of the needs of dyslexic individuals and that their needs are recognised and met.

People sometimes feel that they as an individual alone may not be able to make much of a difference. Nothing could be further from the truth, however, when like minded people come together. When they unite behind a plan to bring about lasting change in society, together the contribution of each individual adds up to a force that can change the world.

Advertising

Index of Advertisers

Notes

Notes